PRAISE FOR HEALING (

"In Healing Civilization, Claudio Naranjo gives us back our once-and-future birthright.... In such seeing, there is the coincidence of opposites, the cessation of contendings, the seeing of all forms in one form, and yes, the resolution and bringing of new light to the long dark night of civilization."

— Jean Houston, author,
A Passion for the Possible, The Possible Human,
A Mythic Life: Learning to Live Our Greater Story;
Program Director, United Nations,
International Institute for Social Artistry; UNICEF advisor

"Claudio Naranjo is one of the most respected pioneers of the human potential movement. His influence has been subtle yet pervasive, and many of the most interesting developments in personal growth can be traced to him. In *Healing Civilization*, he has situated our crisis of civilization in a global and historical context, and presents a stirring call and an exciting foundation for a truly transformative education. His approach is, as always, wise and inspiring because it so clearly emerges from a tremendous depth of personal experience into the far reaches of human possibilities. Claudio Naranjo has made a vital contribution to healing civilization in this perilous time of transition."

— Alfonso Montuori, Professor,
Transformative Studies/Transformative Leadership
California Institute of Integral Studies

"This is a grand theory of Civilization with capital c, denounced as a pathological carrier of patriarchy, with inspiration from a matriarchal past 6,000 years ago or so and promise of a more balanced future. Naranjo works very creatively with the universal Father-Man/Mother-Woman/Son-Daughter-Child triangle and three loves: the agape of the mother, the eros of the child, and father-male love of ideals-ideas. The last one has led to a catastrophic, pathogenic imbalance, with care and love removed. The therapy is to restore mental health: balance among the three loves, to overcome the inner dissociation between thinking, feeling, and doing. This focus on a common factor is a very important factor in the deep culture of civilizations, and a fine way of building the major correlation in violence studies—with gender—into peace studies. Thank you, Claudio!"

— Johan Galtung
Professor of Peace Studies,
Director of Transcend
Recipient of the 1987 Right Livelihood Award
(the "Alternative Nobel Prize")

"In *Healing Civilization*, Claudio Naranjo takes an in-depth and grand vision of humanity in its full historical span, and draws conclusions about the future of our humanity. In this work he gives us some of his overriding insights into the malaise of our contemporary world, an understanding of where this resides and how it functions, and a vision of the way in which our human world may be brought back to a wholesome and integrated way of life.

"There are strikingly original contributions being made here. I leave the joy of this discovery to the reader."

— Mitchell Ginsberg, Ph.D., author,
The Far Shore, The Inner Palace, and *Calm, Clear, and Loving*

"Dr. Naranjo's analysis is brilliant, enlightening, and easy to catch. His integral vision of 'three-brained beings' (thinking, feeling, and doing) offers a profound vision for education in our time."

— Prof. Dr. Heinrich Dauber,
Former Head,
Center for Teacher Education
University of Kassel, Germany

"The great critics of modernity and patriarchy, from Toynbee to Adorno or Foucault, have seldom been able to offer a realistic vision of civilizational alternatives. Claudio Naranjo´s historical anthropology does exactly that. Putting forward the idea that the patriarchal society evolved as a pathological response of humans, as a result of very traumatic conditions in the past, that is no longer functional, Naranjo proposes a socio-therapy of 'the patriarchal mind.' This could only come through an alternative education for the personal and social evolution of humans by balancing and transforming them as 'three brained beings,' starting with the education of the educators themselves. Naranjo's 'culturatry' is a significant contribution towards a science of civilizational healing – and towards a 'politics of civilization' envisioned by the French philosopher Edgar Morin."

— Wilfried Graf, Co-Director,
Institute for Conflict Transformation and Peacebuilding,
Vienna, Austria

"Once again, Claudio Naranjo brings his unique blend of tradition and freshness to bear on the problems and the possibilities of the modern world. His call for an education of love is not only an inspiring ideal, but it finds its practical reality in his now famous SAT curriculum. This inspiring book shows that the transformative education of teachers is the fundamental key to a more humane world. Teachers must not only *know* love, but *be* loving. They cannot simply *talk* about peace, but they must *do* so peacefully."

— John J. Hanagan, Ph.D.
Professor of Comparative Philosophy and Religion
Kansai Gaidai University
Osaka, Japan

"No one who takes Education to heart should miss this work by one who echoes Dewey's conviction that 'if our education is to have meaning for our lives, it should undergo a complete transformation,' and ends his book by stating that 'our future is a race between the transformation of Education and catastrophe.'"

— Pedro Carlos García Arango,
Former Vice-President,
Council of Rectors of Private Universities

"Claudio Naranjo is at the forefront of those seeking to transform the world. For anyone wanting to make a difference for the better, *Healing Civilization* is a must-read!"

— Michael Toms, New Dimensions Radio

"A courageous call by an innovative scholar and successful practitioner in nurturing human potential. This book builds on Claudio Naranjo's earlier works analyzing how human societies suppress individual creativity and potential through their child-rearing and educational practices. Dr. Naranjo points to the pervasive patriarchal structures and mindsets inherited from our distant past—but not inherent in humans. He traces these repressive authoritarian societies and how they overtook earlier matrifocal societies described by Marija Gimbutas and later by Riane Eisler in her *The Chalice and the Blade* and *Sacred Pleasure*.

"Both female and male scholars have noted the repression, fear and aggression leading to violence that is engendered by these patriarchal societies which still pervade humanity world wide.

"I welcome the debate that will be engendered by *Healing Civilization*, as it may help us devise paths toward development and fostering fully-alive, compassionate, empathetic human beings who can evolve toward Planetary Citizenship.

"Dr. Naranjo should take heart that many around the world have taken up the vital task of reforming markets, money-creation, credit-allocation and capitalism itself, to reform markets and grow the new more ecologically and socially aware 'green' companies of the post-fossil fueled Solar Age."

— Hazel Henderson, author,
Ethical Markets: Growing the Green Economy and *Planetary Citizenship: Your Values, Beliefs and Actions Can Shape a Sustainable World*

PRAISE FOR RELATED BOOKS BY CLAUDIO NARANJO

"The peculiarity of Naranjo's approach is that even when his erudite vision is supported in various disciplines, he offers a systemic interpretation of things; it is not simply that of one who knows education, medicine, history, or psychiatry, but one who combines these approaches to present an integrated and complex understanding of reality."

— Juan Casassus,
UNESCO's main expert for Latin America and the Caribbean
[From his Preface to *Changing Education to Change the World*,
Spanish edition]

"Like the prophets, Claudio analyzes lucidly the extremely critical condition of our civilization and identifies its deep root, courageously proposing the only possible cure for ourselves and the Earth: recognizing the 'sin' in our egos, and [in] this way initiating a healing process through education."

— Franco Fabbro,
Dean of the School of Education,
University of Udine, Italy
[From his Preface to *The Patriarchal Ego*, Italian edition]

"Naranjo dissects with unique skill the rotting corpse of Western Civilization, but he doesn't stop at nihilistic disillusion, for his treatment of his themes is permeated with love and compassion and he points at new ways of collective life, sowing hope in the astonished minds of those of us who have been feeling at the edge of an unprecedented historical abyss."

— Alaor Passos, sociologist,
Professor at the University of Brasilia (UnB)

Other Books in English by Claudio Naranjo

The End of Patriarchy and the Dawning of a Tri-Une Society
The One Quest: A Map of the Ways of Transformation*
The Enneagram of Society: Healing the Soul to Heal the World*
Ennea-Type Structures: Self-Analysis for the Seeker*
Enneatypes in Psychotherapy
Transformation through Insight: Enneatypes in Life, Literature and Clinical Practice
The Healing Journey: New Approaches to Consciousness
The Divine Child and the Hero: Inner Meaning in Children's Literature*
How to Be
The Way of Silence and the Talking Cure: On Meditation and Psychotherapy
Character and Neurosis: An Integrative View*
Gestalt Therapy: The Attitude and Practice of an Atheoretical Experientialism
Changing Education to Change the World: A New Vision of Schooling*
My Psychedelic Explorations: The Healing Power and Transformational Potential of Psychoactive Substances
The Revolution We Expected: Cultivating a New Politics of Consciousness
Dionysian Buddhism: Guided Interpersonal Meditations in the Three Yanas
27 Personalities in Search of Being: Experiences of Transformation in the Light of the Enneagram (in preparation, 2022)*

* Published by Gateways Books and Tapes

HEALING
CIVILIZATION

HEALING
CIVILIZATION

BRINGING PERSONAL TRANSFORMATION INTO THE SOCIETAL REALM
THROUGH EDUCATION AND THE INTEGRATION OF THE INTRA-PSYCHIC FAMILY

CLAUDIO NARANJO

FOREWORD TO THE AMERICAN EDITION
BY JEAN HOUSTON

Rose Press / Gateways Books and Tapes
Oakland, CA / Nevada City, CA

Published by Rose Press / Gateways Books and Tapes

Rose Press
www.rosepress.com
rosepressbooks@yahoo.com

Gateways Books and Tapes, P.O. Box 370, Nevada City, CA 95959
www.gatewaysbooksandtapes.com

First American edition. Published 2010. Reprinted 2022.
Printed in the United States of America
17 16 15 14 13 12 11 10   1 2 3 4 5
ISBN #: 978-0-89556-163-3

Library of Congress Cataloging-in-Publication Data

Naranjo, Claudio.
  Healing civilization : bringing personal transformation into the
  societal realm through education and the integration of the
  intra-psychic family / Claudio Naranjo ; foreword to the
  English-Language edition by Jean Houston. ~ English-language ed.
     p. cm.
  Includes bibliographical references and index.
  ISBN 978-0-89556-163-3
  1. Patriarchy. 2. Patriarchy~Religious aspects. 3. Social structure.
  I. Title.
  GN479.6.N38 2010
  306~dc22

                              2009038701

Editor & Publisher: Naomi Rose
Cover illustration: Jaclyne Scardova
Cover design: Design Site
Interior book design, proofreading, research: Gabriel Steinfeld
Design consultation, typesetting, production: Paula Hendricks, Cinnabar Bridge
Additional research: David Carr, Moving Words
Index: Mary Harper, Access Points Indexing

"Political, economic or social revolutions are not the answer, since they have led to terrible tyrannies or simple changes in power and authority of a different group. Such revolutions are never the way out of the confusion and inner conflict in which we live.

But there is a revolution that is different, and it *must* come about if we are to emerge from the interminable series of anxieties, conflicts and frustrations in which we are caught. This revolution must begin not with theoretical conceptions, which in the long run prove to be ineffective, but with a radical change of the mind itself. Such a transformation could only come about through a correct education and the full development of human beings."

— J. Krishnamurti, *The Art of Living*

CONTENTS

FOREWORD

TO THE AMERICAN EDITION

JEAN HOUSTON

He does not know it, but I have been observing the journey of Claudio Naranjo for the better part of forty years. And what I have seen is a man who encompasses the Realities from the scientific to the shamanic. Scholar, poet of the possible, he is an explorer of the outer reaches of inner space. His depth soundings of the wells of history and civilization resound with the echo of one who hears the pathology while seeking the song of the new mythos of who we are, where we have been, and what we yet can be. Hundreds of years ago, he would have been both priest and alchemist. Today, in this luminous work, *Healing Civilization*, he takes on the dark issue that is the cause of so many of our discontents — the patriarchal origins of civilization. Seeking balance he recalls the matristic period, when women's values were critical to the weave of cultures.

As the remarkable, if highly controversial, work of Marija Gimbutas and others has shown, the culture of old Europe from about 7000 to 3500 B.C. was essentially a Neolithic agrarian economy centering around the rites and worship of the Great Goddess. The findings of archaeologists James Mellaart in Catal Huyuk in Turkey and of Gimbutas in southeastern Europe reveal civilizations of extremely complex and sophisticated arts, crafts, technology, and social organization. Further, as advocates of these findings such as Riane Eisler suggest, the evidence seems to indicate that these were basically non-patriarchal partnership societies, with descent and inheritance passed through the mother, and with women playing key roles in all aspects of life and work.

What was it like to live in these cultures governed by the Goddess archetype? In all likelihood, the emphasis was on being rather than doing, on deepening rather than producing and achieving. Process was more important than product, for the Great Goddess was pre-eminently a deity of process, of the natural rhythms of life and their unfolding in the cycles that govern nature. Thus, she was worshipped for her many aspects — as Earth Mother; guarantor of fertility; guardian of childbirth; protector and sustainer of growth in children, crops, and animals; as healer, helper, and source of inspiration and creativity; and as the Lady of the Beasts, lady of arts and poetry, and ruler of death.

Most important of all, her ways were ones of peace. Thus, in the period under consideration, the art is non-heroic; indeed, there are no representations of heroes, conquests, or captives — that came much later. Instead, the art abounds with scenes and symbols from nature — Sun and water, serpents, birds and butterflies — and everywhere shrines, votive offerings, images, and figurines of the Goddess. The artistic emphasis is never on the straight line but on the meander and the spiral, implying the many turnings of the dance of life. All in all, one gains the impression of a gentle, high culture — nurturing, playful, and pacific.

This culture was exported to Crete, where it flourished in populous well-organized cities, multistoried palaces, networks of fine roads, productive farms, an almost modern system of drainage and irrigation works, a rich economy with high living standards, and the lively and joyous artistic style so characteristic of Cretan life and sensibility. Again, certain scholars suggest that this was a culture of male-female equality and partnership; and again too, the spiritual authority and guiding principles were those of the Great Goddess. Here the Goddess was seen in her triple manifestation, with her shape-shifting finding its correspondence in the seasons and the phases of the Moon. Thus, she appears as maiden (spring/the new Moon), fertile mother (summer and fall/the waxing and full Moon), and wise old one (winter/the waning Moon).

The Goddess in her threefold form is found the world over in myth, theology, legend, and literature. In ancient Greece she appears in many goddess triads, perhaps the best known being her disclosure in the Eleusinian Mysteries as mother (Demeter), daughter (Persephone), and the wise one of magic (Hecate). In Arthurian legend, she appears as the maidenly Lady of the Lake who gives Arthur his sword; as his wife Guinevere; and as his magical half-sister, Morgan le Fay.

In both the earlier and later civilizations of Greece, Athena personified an aspect of the Triple Goddess in her role as patroness of arts, crafts, and sciences. Charlene Spretnak, in her study of pre-Hellenic goddesses, offers a beautiful meditation on the myth of Athena that describes perfectly this earlier role of the Goddess in the matristic cultures:

In the Minoan days of Crete an unprecedented flowering of learning and the arts was cultivated by Athena. Dynamic architecture rose to four stories, pillared and finely detailed, yet always infused with the serenity of the Goddess. Patiently Her mortals charted the heavens, devised a calendar, kept written archives. In the palaces they painted striking frescoes of Her Priestesses and sculpted Her owl and ever-renewing serpent in the shrine rooms. Goddess figures and their rituals were deftly engraved on seals and amulets. Graceful scenes were cast in relief for gold vessels and jewelry. Athena nurtured all the arts, but Her favorites were weaving and pottery.

Long before there were palaces, the Goddess had appeared to a group of women gathering plants in a field. She broke open the stems of blue-flowered flax and showed them how the threadlike fibers could be spun and then woven. The woof and warp danced in Her fingers until a length of cloth was born before them. She told them which plants and roots would color the cloth, and then She led the mortals from the field to a pit of clay. There they watched Athena form a long serpent and coil it, much like the serpents coiled around Her arms. She formed a vessel and smoothed the sides, then deftly applied a paste made from another clay and water. When it was baked in a hollow in the earth, a spiral pattern emerged clearly. The image of circles that repeat and repeat yet move forward was kept by the women for centuries.

As the mortals moved forward, Athena guided the impulse of the arts. She knew they would never flourish in an air of strife, so She protected households from divisive forces and guarded towns against aggression. So invincible was the aura of Her protection that the Minoans lived in unfortified coastal towns. Their shipping trade prospered and they enjoyed a peace that spanned a thousand years. To Athena each family held the olive bough sacred, each worshipped Her in their home. Then quite suddenly the flowering of the Minoans was slashed. Northern barbarians, more fierce than the Aegean Goddess had ever known, invaded the island and carried Athena away to Attica. There they made her a soldier.[1]

These gentle civilizations perished at the hands of the marauding bands of invaders, the latest in the long line of Indo-Aryan warrior nomads. These conquerors not only imposed their own rigid rules but also shattered the finely wrought symbiosis among humans, nature, culture, and spiritual realities. Their consciousness divided, their loyalties uncertain, the invaders felt both drawn to and terrified by the gentle complexity of the high civilizations in which they found themselves. They were both fascinated and frightened by the pervasiveness of its eroticisms. Thus, they muscled and armored themselves against the enticement of its sensualities. They feared, dreaded, and violated the places and persons who bore witness to the ongoing communication between the seen and unseen orders, which they themselves had long since lost.

We see a late version of this in the *Iliad*, when the holy communicant and prophetess, Cassandra, is ravaged on the altar of Athena. Thus, to maintain his separateness, the patriarchal hero-invader — in Greece, in India, and in the Fertile Crescent — dreads the caress. When he comes close, it is only to subdue by duel or rape.

Not that these invaders failed to adopt many of the ways and skills of the more ancient cultures. The Achaeans, for example, assimilated much of the Minoan culture. But they did so by tearing out the feminine threads in the cultural tapestry, leaving a ragged social fabric that was missing many pieces. The suppression of the rich and complex feminine characteristics of the goddess Athena is typical of this rending of culture and consciousness. Too powerful a spiritual force to remove, she is instead pre-empted by the Achaean patriarchy to become Daddy's girl, the spirit of Zeus, born shrieking a harrowing cry that frightens even the gods as she emerges fully armored from the top of his head.

One wonders what lay in this cry. Was it perhaps the cry of outrage of one forced to live a lie, to inhabit a projection? This is hard enough for humans; one can only imagine how devastating it must be for divinity. Caught in the dreams of the long dark night of the heroic ages of Mycenean power and might, Athena is constrained to be a warrior goddess and protector of the citadels of power.

But one can never contain an archetype for long — certainly not one of such antiquity and complexity. Even when she is raging through the *Iliad*, her deeper nature is there in potentia. And in the *Odyssey*, she is clearly in transition. All her acts attest to this shift, which explains all her changes, her disguises, her transformings. Her transition is not only to grow beyond the patriarchal heroic image thrust upon her and to acquire again some of the fuller dimensions she had in earlier times, but also to become something more — a goddess who transcends both the Minoan and Mycenean visions of her, a goddess of transformation who partners the evolutionary journey of both individuals and culture. For Athena, what had been seeded in Minoan culture seems to emerge again after many centuries of being kept in the dark of the patriarchal heroic brain. With the *Odyssey*, she emerges as a transpersonal and transformational goddess: no longer merely the patron of imperial adventure, but now the guiding spirit who helps refine and deepen the culture of the homeplace.

I mention the journey of Athena because it gives substance to Naranjo's argument about the necessity for the rise of the feminine in value and in deed, if we are to survive the challenges of the next years.

I have worked in over 100 countries for the United Nations and other international agencies training leaders in human development in the light of social change, especially in developing countries. I call this work social artistry, for — as with artistic creations — it requires the skills of dedication, focus, stick-to-it-ness, and aesthetic passion. The canvas is the social canvas, and its practitioners learn to cross the great divide of otherness and engage in radical empathy in order to help preserve culture, accomplish Millennium development goals, and midwife the emerging new story.

In every country I visit, I find that 70 percent and more of those who take the initiative to make a difference and follow through on their social projects are Athena-like women of a "certain age." Enjoying post-menopausal zest, theirs is a larger caring, a deeper commitment to social change and community betterment. Hands-on, sensory-rich, vibrant with laughter and intelligence, they get the job done while educating the young ones in ways that Naranjo would find exhilarating. They are the precursors of the pragmatic aspect of the rising feminine, living antidotes to the folly and fallout of the patriarchal ages.

What I find in them is the ability to look at the openings, the places where cultures can meet and exchange the skills and discoveries that had been uniquely theirs but now can belong to the whole planetary condition. They are mindful of the planet Herself and the plan that She and the cosmic forces may have in mind for us. Above all is their sense of the great spiritual connectedness within, among, and beyond all peoples, regardless of their cultural or religious differences.

In this regard, we see the growing planetization as more important, in some ways, than the globalization that gets so much attention. Globalization belongs to the patriarchal era, in that it supports the corporate hegemony of the world, a kind of corporate colonialism. Planetization, on the other hand, is of a more feminine nature in that it is relational — the world-mind taking a walk with itself. The gradual decline of the nation state is only a part of this; the clash of civilizations or of contending patriarchies may be the sunset effect of the older orders, not the thing to come — although, like the setting sun, it is growing much brighter and more spectacular as it approaches the horizon. At the same time, with everything in transition, the matristic values affirm that we can no longer afford to live as remedial members of the human race. With the rising feminine, a new set of values — holistic, syncretic, relationship- and process-oriented, organic, spiritual — is rising within us and around us. And though the forces of entropy and fear seek to contain or regress us, we know there is no going back. Our complex time requires a wiser use of our capacities, a richer music from the instrument we have been given.

The world will thrive only if we can grow. The possible society will become a reality only if we learn to be the possible humans we are capable of being. This requires the new balance between masculine and feminine consciousness. The post-civilizational intelligence that could arise from this will cause us to take initiatives that, in patriarchal ages, would have seemed unlikely, if not impossible. But now, in the last few years, the world has been rearranged; the reset button of history has been hit.

But what to do? Where to go? How to take initiative? And — what is key here — how to understand our new role and purpose in this most compelling moment in human history, when what we do will make a difference as to whether we grow or die?

Many of the spiritual teachers of the world have likened our lives to "a sleep and a forgetting." The life and work of Claudio Naranjo is predicated on awakening, on going off-robot and abandoning lackluster passivity to engage co-creation with vigor, attention, focus, and radiance. Thus, the life he envisions, once the genders return to balance, can be perhaps the greatest accelerator of evolutionary enhancement. Through this happening, we tap into wider physical, mental, and emotional systems, and thus gain entrance into the next stage of our unfolding, both individually and collectively. Perhaps the purpose of evolution is to grow us into co-creators who can play a conscious role in transforming the potentialities inherent in matter and ideas into new forms, better societies, richer meanings, and high art.

In *Healing Civilization*, Claudio Naranjo gives us back our once-and-future birthright, as together, male and female, we have the potential to come into phase with the creative energies of the universe and our scope to enlarge, such that everything we see — the little girl in the swing, the dog gnawing a bone, the old man in the nursing home, the snappy clerk at the check-out counter — becomes a celebration of the wild, exuberant, all-accomplishing energy of spirited manifestation. In such partnership, we participate in the vigor and the generosity of Divine Life.

We would hope that as a result of Naranjo's evocative manifesto, readers will begin to look at each other from newly engendered gender-seeing, experiencing one another as transparent to transcendence, the life force in its infinite oscillations. In such seeing, we will be able to see one another's possibilities with a natural felicity we had not known before. And in such seeing, there is the coincidence of opposites, the cessation of contendings, the seeing of all forms in one form, and yes, the resolution and bringing of new light to the long dark night of civilization.

— Jean Houston

Dr. Jean Houston is long regarded as one of the principal founders of the Human Potential Movement. A scholar, philosopher, and researcher in human capacities, her myriad contributions include: co-founding The Foundation for Mind Research and a modern Mystery School; founding The Possible Society; working with the United Nations as Program Director of the International Institute for Social Artistry, and advisor to UNICEF in human and cultural development; and more. She has served in an advisory capacity to the Dalai Lama, then-President William Clinton and Mrs. Clinton, and former President Jimmy Carter and Mrs. Carter, and has counseled leaders at similar levels in many countries and cultures. A recipient of numerous honors, including the Lifetime Outstanding Creative Achievement Award from the Creative Education Foundation, Houston is the author of 25 books, including A Passion for the Possible, Search for the Beloved, Life Force, The Possible Human, A Mythic Life: Learning to Live Our Greater Story, *and* Manual for a Peacemaker. *Her widely viewed PBS special, "A Passion for the Possible," called on human beings to consider their potential and greatness.*

INTRODUCTION

ARNO VOGEL

My encounter with this book was magic, if by this word we were to designate the conviction — deeply rooted in the human soul since the beginning of time, and perhaps for all time — that chance does not exist. I had set forth to meet Claudio seeking counsel for the difficult transition that separates one cycle of life that is closing from another that has not yet commenced. I could not even have imagined, then, that I was setting forth, also, to meet *Healing Civilization*.

The first glimpses of the text, in the author's company, were enough to convince me that I had a very special work before my eyes. Thus, I tried to accept, resolutely and with great joy, the invitation to write this Introduction — a task that seemed at once not only honorable, but also exciting and challenging.

The true dimension of the challenge, however, would only reveal itself to me later on, in front of a comprehensive version of the text. I experienced the same sensation of fascination as with the first book, but now it was accompanied by a startling quality that was impossible to disguise. I had difficulty in discovering the motive of my innumerable doubts. I managed to detect it, finally, through my subsequent re-readings, during which I made an effort to find possible objections or contributions to the book's data and theory.

In truth, I had been lacking, until then, the adequate focus that what Claudio presents to us here is an essay — brilliant and incisive. In it he formulates, with great daring and enviable erudition, an Anthropology, in the precise sense of the word: that is, an attempt to respond to the great (and eternal) question as to what, finally, is Man, in his essence and destiny.

In this sense, many passages of *Healing Civilization* could lead to complementary and illustrative commentaries and references, and, eventually, debates or observations, some of them polemic. Meanwhile, I think all this comes from the very nature of the genre, for any essay worthy of the name must venture beyond the frontiers of existing knowledge — being, therefore, obliged to take risks, advancing hypotheses for which analytical developments capable of verifying (or falsifying) them are still unavailable.

As Jorge Luis Borges' character, Inspector Lönnrot, affirms, reality has no obligation whatsoever to be interesting. Hypotheses, on the contrary, cannot do without such a quality. And here is something that this book, certainly, will provide its reader — the opportunity to reflect, argue, query not only the text in its multiple implications but, above all, oneself, confronting what is being read with one's most essential experiences.

Another outstanding aspect of the essay is the tone of its discourse: at times rather hard and unrelenting, without ever

becoming pamphletary — "without ever losing tenderness," as
is fitting for thought centered on Love, that great, inherent, essential value to human being and existing. Love — the essential
principle of positive reciprocity, in any of its forms — which
furthermore requires the courage and determination of a con-
stant quest, and which may only be reached at the cost of an
ever-renewed effort. Although the goodness and joy of being
pertain to the human essence, their realization will demand,
invariably, overcoming one's self — whether an individual or
collective one-self — which insists on maintaining submission
to the mechanical inertia of its active unconscious, as G. I.
Gurdjieff so well observed when discussing Man's "possible"
evolution.

The full comprehension of this "human tragedy," with all
its complications, is precisely what justifies the severe delivery,
at times on the verge of harshness, of *Healing Civilization*. The
voice in which it makes itself heard reminded me, during the
course of my readings, of the tone of the prophets of the Old
Testament. In fact, its objective, like theirs, is not so much
that of predicting the future, painted with the strong colors of
pedagogic disillusion. It is, first and perhaps above all, that of
unleashing a more propitious metamorphosis of human society
— whether for the survival of the species or the full affirmation
of the individuals of which it is composed.

The prophetic voice announces a new era of humanity,
in which the present one, having finally recouped the "principles and precepts of return to the evidence," will recognize
in its thoughts and deeds the founding and constitutive triad
of its nature, both biological and social — Man, Woman, and
Child; Father, Mother, and Son/Daughter; Law, Emotion, and
Instinct. Whoever realizes all this may not only reconcile with
the intonation of the text and, in a general way, with the style

of the discourse, but also come to appreciate its strategic necessity and its subtle handling, indispensable to the conception and execution of the essay itself.

Likewise, I faced with difficulty what seemed at certain moments to reach the edge of a demonization of the masculine principle — until I realized that Claudio only rejects its perversion, its imbalance, its lack of measure: the foolish pre-eminence (and arrogance) which this principle has acquired throughout the centuries since Classical Antiquity. In this sense, from among all the partial pieces that compose *Healing Civilization*, the text dedicated to the "patriarchal mind" is the one that I believe absolutely unalterable.

In another moment, I thought to have found an unjustifiable idealization of the feminine. Yet later, my eyes opened and I discerned that what was in question here was also the principle — that is, the basis and order, more than its eventual ethnological and historical updating. Apropos of which, a verse by Goethe from Faust, Part Two came to mind: "*Das ewig Weibliche zieht uns hinan*" — "The Eternal Feminine leads us on." It is precisely this that is being addressed, here! It is a matter of penetrating, once again, the heavy veils of blindness and deafness of anthropological science, which — completely entangled in a "Faustian" modernity — knows not how to hear the naturalist and poet; which has cast Bachofen's *The Mother* right into oblivion, throwing out the matriarchy with the bathwater of evolutionism; and which has ignored *The White Goddess* of Robert Graves, this erudite and attentive reader of Frazer, one of his venerable founding fathers.

With *Healing Civilization*, Claudio Naranjo most definitely takes his place among the great critics of modernity. Many of those voices had expressed their conviction of the modern world going against progressive optimisms of all shades, corresponding to a "dark age." Beyond this, Claudio achieves what is most difficult: he links the soberest and severest of diagnoses with the most perennial and tender hope of the possible advent of an age of harmony among the elements of the human trinity — Father, Mother, and Child — as reconciled poles of the individual and of society.

Healing Civilization is, in every sense, a book capable of enrapturing its readers, not only for its power of synthesis, analytic acuity, and rhetorical astuteness, but even more so for its refined symbolic ear — qualities which, in each paragraph of this remarkable composition, distinguish and legitimize both the work and the author.

— Arno Vogel

Campos dos Goytacazes/Rio de Janeiro

January 20, 2007

Arno Vogel, Associate Professor of Anthropology at the State University of Norte Fluminense Darcy Ribeiro, Brazil, was formerly Director of FLACSO (Facultad Latinoamericana de Ciencias Sociales).

A PRELIMINARY NOTE

THIS BOOK ORIGINATED AS I was updating a previous one, *The End of Patriarchy*, which Juanjo Herrera, former cultural attaché at the Spanish Embassy in Russia, encouraged me to revise in view of our global times and my recent involvement in the transformation of education. I accepted; yet as I wrote, I discarded the older writing and in the end produced an over-sized document that I decided to divide into two. The result was a book entitled *The Patriarchal Ego* (to be released this year in Italy by Urra) and the present volume (already published in Italy by Franco Angeli), originally entitled *Civilization – A Curable Disease*.

In Chapter 1, "A Complex Problematique and Its Silenced Root," I begin this book by stating the idea that it is time to realize that what we call civilization — which is to say, patriarchal society — falls short of civilization proper, and should be regarded as a pathological and now destructively obsolete response of humans to very traumatic conditions in the past.

Next, in Chapter 2, "Tótila Albert and His Vision of a Tri-une Society," I speak of the person who — as early as the 1930s — denounced patriarchy as the root of all our social ills. It was through him that I learned not only about patriarchy's obsolete barbarism, but also about his vision of a healthy alternative.

In Chapter 3, "Civilization as Hubris," I continue with a reflection on the origins of civilization. I propose that not only was civilization born from a great light, but that it was also affected by the darkness cast by that great light: a transformation of the appreciation of greatness into narcissistic grandiosity that was part of the shift from a matristic culture to patriarchy in the mythical age of heroes.

After this, in Chapter 4, "Patriarchy Today," I explore the characteristics of present patriarchal society, showing the progressive deterioration of life, environment, culture, and human communities that takes place as attachment to an obsolete patriarchy becomes increasingly deadly.

Then, in Chapter 5, "The Patriarchal Mind," I begin by briefly presenting my notion of mental health and self-realization as a balance among the three loves characteristic of the three inner persons (Father, Mother, and Child) — a balance made possible by the wisdom of neutral, or detached, awareness. In light of this conception, I further reflect on the social pathology that I call the patriarchal mind, examining this collective condition as a state of inner disassociation among thinking, feeling, and doing; an obscuration of awareness; and a subordination of eros (characteristic of the Inner Child) and agape (characteristic of Mother-love) to a love of ideals that is the echo of Father-love.

Next, in Chapter 6, "The Alternative to Patriarchy," I present a chronology of libertarian ideas, and also spell out more elaborately Tótila Albert's vision of full humanness as a triple embrace in the human psyche among the three "inner persons," the experiential counterparts of the three human brains.

Chapter 7, "A Tri-focal Education to Transcend Patriarchy," begins by pointing out the need to place the fostering of human growth as the highest priority, and the unique potential of education to turn the tide of history. It then goes on to present a more specific blueprint of what a balanced — and balancing — education for "three-brained beings" could be.

Finally, Chapter 8, "Healing Teachers to Transform Education," discusses how teachers might be prepared to overhaul patriarchal education in favor of a transformative education for both personal and social evolution, and describes the evolution of my own work with groups and the method I now offer as a supplement to the traditional education of teachers.

I have ended the book with an Epilogue, which in turn ends with the book's dedication to Tótila Albert, the person whom I may call my spiritual father, and whose influence has been for me a guiding light.

Writing this book has been an impassioned activity, and I hope that my creative enthusiasm will be echoed in the enthusiasm with which it is read and in the good that it does. The things I talk about in it are familiar to my friends and students, but not to the wide audience that I expect to reach through the written word. I very much hope that, like my book *Changing Education to Change the World* (presently in circulation in Spanish, Italian, and Portuguese versions), *Healing Civilization* may interest the human community in putting our presently conservative school systems in the service of personal and social evolution.

I would be very glad if I could interest the potentates of the world in the notion that our future is in their hands, and that it is within their power to launch the initiative of becoming our saviors by changing patriarchal education into transformative education. For I think that only this could allow us to change the course of the seemingly inevitable tide of history.

— Claudio Naranjo
Berkeley, California

CHAPTER 1

A COMPLEX *PROBLEMATIQUE* AND ITS SILENCED ROOT

Patriarchy and misogyny persist in every major contemporary society [as perusing the daily news confirms]. From the Taliban in Afghanistan to Japanese men's repression of women, from male pro-life fanatics in the United States to the practice of bride burning in India, evidence for these invidious twins abounds. Wide swaths of Africa and the Islamic world still practice female genital mutilation. Forced prostitution is rife among the former Soviet republics, and sex slavery is an ugly fact of life from Saudi Arabia to Thailand.

Humanity staggers on like a person who has suffered a stroke that left half the body paralyzed. The masculine half of the body politic resists acknowledging the obvious: Disdaining, ignoring and dismissing its distaff half is extremely counter-productive. Until individuals, couples, and cultures can facilitate and appreciate the contributions of both halves of the

human psyche, the human species will continue to
be hobbled by this serious handicap.[1]

— Leonard Shlain

THE MALAISE OF A CIVILIZATION IN CRISIS

THAT CIVILIZATION IS IN CRISIS has become obvious. And yet
this is not a new situation. Less than a century ago, in Freud's
final book, *Civilization and Its Discontents*, he proposed that
civilization's malaise was the inevitable consequence of its
incompatibility with human nature, and therefore with health
and happiness.

Over many years, Freud's pessimism has come under criticism — not only regarding what is possible for the future, but
also mainly regarding the natural goodness of human beings.
Yet as we enter the third millennium, we cannot help but
appreciate the truth that his great prophetic mind perceived
with a lucidity unshadowed by the sentimentalism of the common man: that civilization as we know it is incompatible with
health, and will continue to be so in its current form.

Yes: Human nature — which mythic language wisely de-
clares to have been created in God's *image and likeness* — is
incompatible with civilization, which is intrinsically anti-in-
stinctive and pathogenic. But also, no: for humanity will *not*
be incapable of transcending the form of collective living that
was adopted at the turn of the Bronze Age — a form that even
now is transmitted through the generations to its descendants.
And we have reason to hope that the implicit goodness of human nature — once it has been at least partially liberated from
the prison of its blindness and millennial evil, and can leave
its obsolete institutions and modes of thinking behind — may

finally evolve towards a beneficial coexistence and actually find that happiness prophesied by the great spiritual traditions of antiquity.

As a professional dedicated to assisting the therapeutic and spiritual evolution of individuals, I have witnessed countless examples of how people embark on a process of transformation by becoming aware of themselves, aided by appropriate intention and effort. This process, given sufficient time and application, progressively deactivates the conditioned, pathogenic childhood personality. Beyond even that, it may lead to the emergence of a deeper level of awareness than that of thinking, emotions, desires, or sensations: a more profound awareness, in which the experience of *being* and the felt meaning of life have their foundation. Although this constitutes our true nature, in our so-called *civilized* condition it ordinarily lies in a darkened, or veiled, condition — as if asleep.

My experience as a therapist working with groups over the last three decades has nurtured not only my trust in the intrinsic goodness of humans and in the individual's possibility of leaving destructiveness behind, but also my hope in *collective* transformation. And now that humanity is undergoing a planetary crisis, I must admit to being *apocalyptic* — if by this one means a person who hopes that, in spite of the life-or-death dimension of our crisis, we have what we need within us to ensure that it will not be a fatal one.

Many civilizations have risen and faded away, as Arnold J. Toynbee has well argued, and others (like our own) have been transformed through something akin to hybridization. But there is yet to be a *civilization* that undergoes the death-and-rebirth process that we have come to recognize as the essence of *individual* transformation, as manifest through the experience of those who have completed it: the prophets, enlightened individuals, and mythic heroes. In light of this vision, let us hope that the decaying structure of Western Christian civilization learns to die well, so that the regeneration of our social body may take place under the best of possible conditions.

How can we *not* hope for such a collective death-and-re-birth, when the commercial interests of the powerful devastate our environment, our values, our quality of life, our education, our culture, and even life itself?

And how can we not hope that the destruction of life and the human mind, to date, will at least stimulate awareness, and thus accelerate a regenerative process — in the same way that diseases indirectly cause their own cure by stimulating the organism's defenses. Funny as it may sound, the California author and spiritual teacher, E. J. Gold, did not find it at all absurd to write (in a 1980s humor magazine), "As Brother Rabbit said, maybe civilization is nature's way of telling us to slow down."

Yes, the rhythm of life speeds up as civilization advances. And it would seem that we have no more time left for listening to the voices of the past. The very rhythm of civilization's growth seems to be gathering speed, and we feel it sweep us away in its impetuous current. Civilization even seems to feed on our energies like a cancer, without delivering the satisfactions that we expected from its progress.

It was during the mid-1960s — a cultural turning point — that I first wrote about the twilight of patriarchal civilization. The rise of a new consciousness was in the foreground, expressed through therapeutic revolution, feminism, ecology, the defense of civil rights and democratic values, and other libertarian initiatives. At the same time, however, a cultural death was also taking place: the essence of the counter-culture involved the desire to leave behind old forms of life and obsolete solutions.

Yet the new anti-authoritarianism of the sixties seemed only the most recent stage of a revolutionary process that first began in the Renaissance, continued during the Reformation, and blossomed during the Enlightenment (with the weakening of the Old Regime, the rise of the bourgeoisie, and the independence of the American colonies). This progression was to culminate in Nietzsche, whose statement "God is dead" reflected the quest for a spiritual truth beyond the forms and language of traditional religion.

However, it has only been since the 1980s that the darker aspect of our collective death-and-rebirth has emerged into the foreground. Indeed, this cultural death is evident not only in our loss of values and in the degradation of wisdom into mere information, but also in the generalized devaluation of our earlier points of reference. Much of the Western world's population is now disenchanted with governments, authorities, experts, ideologies, and even science and philosophy, not to mention religions. The cynicism of the times is mirrored in a total relativism that finds voice in the writings of the post-modern thinkers, who not only observe the world's disenchantment but also share in it. Surely, such total relativism has been a response to violence, stupidity, and injustice, and reflects a greater understanding of history. Perhaps it may even be viewed as a good thing, in light of our need to free ourselves from the chains of a past that still conditions us, even as we boast that we have left all ideology behind.

For it is evident that during the last few decades, when our collective situation has grown more critical than ever, the ideological pendulum has swung towards a new conservatism, in which conformity again prevails over the ever-rising popular impulse towards change. And although the societal illness continues, the dissonance between facts and opinions has lent it a new flavor: it deals with a vague *malaise* — a vague suspicion that we are sinking and there is nothing we can do about it.

Our civilization is indeed dying, at the same time that millions are spent on the art of distraction. The communications media is used to deceive us into feeling that everything is okay, and that our problems will be resolved via technology.

Yet more than just our civilization is threatened. If we persist in our way of living, over the course of a limited number of generations our abused planet will barely allow a small fraction of our present human population to survive. Still, we hardly react. Individual interests in profit seem to prevail, far beyond people's interest in the common good. "Every man for himself" is today's prevailing stance, as before an impending shipwreck.

I believe that much of our collective impotence derives from hopelessness. And this hopelessness, itself, derives from a lack of true perception. We do not see what lies at the heart of our problems — and, correspondingly, what we can do to remedy our critical predicament.

It is the contention of this book that the root of our social problems has not been properly understood, and that therefore politics is much like the field of medicine, before scientific discoveries were made enabling physicians to properly diagnose infectious diseases and prescribe the corresponding cures. To better explain what this analogy means, I invite you to turn with me now to a consideration of our multi-faceted *problematique.*[2] This will provide a springboard for my thesis concerning the diagnosis of humanity's fundamental, yet obscured, social problem.

IN MEDIAS RES

"IT IS unforgivable that so many problems from the past are still with us, absorbing vast energies and resources desperately needed for nobler purposes," said U Thant (then-Secretary-General of the United Nations) as early as 1970, on the occasion of that organization's twenty-fifth anniversary. After reviewing some of these "problems from the past" — such as the armaments race, racism, violations of human rights, and *"dreams of power and domination instead of fraternal coexistence,"* he observed that:

> While these antiquated concepts and attitudes persist, the rapid pace of change around us breeds new problems which cry for the world's collective attention and care: the increasing discrepancy between rich and poor nations, the scientific and technological gap, the population explosion, the deterioration of the environment, the urban proliferation, the drug problem, the alienation of youth, the excessive consumption of resources by insatiable societies and institutions. The very survival of a civilized and humane society seems to be at stake.[3]

In addition to these problems, another (later emphasized by the pioneering Club of Rome) has emerged in the modern world: in our contemporary scenario, the multiplicity of world-wide problems have such complex interrelations that the very measures which could solve any one of these inevitably lead to the aggravation of another. Even simply attending to one issue may involve a selective inattention to the rest.

It has been recognized that the situation requires an inter-
disciplinary approach, which has come into vogue worldwide.
Yet beyond this, I believe it is important to *attend to the heart
of the macro-problem*: the fundamental ill from which the diverse
aspects of our problematique derive, in much the same way
that different bodily symptoms are, at base, manifestations of
the same disease.

Of course, there are those who think that we need not
overcomplicate something that is really much simpler. Particularly from 1980 onwards, what could be called a "global capital-
ist empire" has been established under the banner of neo-liberalism, the result of which has been the catastrophic destruction
of the environment and the increasing poverty of people,
in direct correlation with the progressive wealth of nations.

In our day and age, as discussions increasingly turn to
the subject of crisis, it is clear that the forces of international
business and the power of money[4] hold sway over the political world and the sovereign states. Decisions concerning the
well being of society are no longer in the hands of its heads
of state. Instead, they largely hinge on big trans-national businesses, which operate with the sole aim of optimizing their
profits. It would therefore be very tempting to say that our
current disease is simply what ancient translations of the Gospel used to call *Mammon*. (These days, we speak of *money*; but
earlier it was personified, as in the saying, "No man can serve
two masters, both God and Mammon.")

Indeed, one cannot serve both the cause of love and the
cause of profit at the same time. However, I think that emphasizing the economic issue distracts us from the fact that
*the commercialization of the world – and of life – is only one facet
of a more complex problematique*. The whole of our main ills
— including such excesses as violence, injustice, corruption,

authoritarianism, and others — has derived from a common root: a *neglected* root that has gone unattended until now, just as we have failed to look at our psychological ills.

It is my conviction that all such ills are manifestations of the *patriarchal organization of both the human mind and of society*.

Before we examine the consequences of this viewpoint, let us pause a moment to reflect on the meaning of the word *patriarchal*. It is a word that was first introduced by a Swiss historian, Johann Bachofen — a contemporary and colleague of Nietzsche at the University of Basel — who is remembered as the discoverer of our remote "matriarchal" past.

At the end of the nineteenth century, Bachofen discovered the existence of ancient cultures vastly different from ours in terms of aspects previously considered to be intrinsic to human nature (such as personal dominance). Today, archaeological excavations have proven the accuracy of his intuitive interpretation[5] of Herodotus' reports on some ancient peoples (such as the Lybians). Since then, many anthropologists — as farfetched as the hypothesis of a "matriarchy" first seemed to them — have examined living primitive cultures and found that *matrism* was indeed pervasive.

We need to recognize Bachofen had assumed that before the rise of male dominance there was a situation of female dominance, characterized by the explicit prominence of women leaders. When this was found to be a rare situation among primitive cultures, ethnologists felt that their search for matriarchy had been mistaken. In time, however, it came to be understood that feminine power generally is not expressed through dominance by *women*, but by the dominance of feminine *values*: community, cooperation, cultivation, and, more broadly, life. This is why the term *matristic*, introduced by Marija Gimbutas, has come into use today. Personal dominance being a male trait, the matristic spirit has been expressed through the power of the group, giving priority to relationships, and the ascendancy of the community spirit — the bonds of caring.

If the excess of patriarchy is *individual* tyranny, then we can say that the excess of matristic culture was *group* tyranny. Apart from the precarious struggle for survival that the great drought ensuing from the last glacial period represented (which could account for a culture of competition), we can imagine that male dominance — instilled some five or six thousand years ago, and bringing with it a predominance of warring values over loving values — entailed a rebellion against such community tyranny in the early Neolithic era.

Some academics seem to resist the notion that patriarchal aggression is cultural and historical, rather than genetic. Yet I find ample reason to think that the so-called *fall* of man was an historical event — a consequence of survival difficulties that forced the first sedentary communities to become depredatory, violent, and insensitive. Dr. James DeMeo has established a correlation between desertification, famine and starvation, and patristic attitudes, based on data from over 1,100 studies of different cultures in the area that he designates as "Saharasia." He proposes that it is in "desertification," the turning of fertile lands into deserts, that the traumatic origin of patriarchy lies:

> With very few exceptions, there is no clear or unambiguous evidence for warfare or social violence anywhere on planet Earth prior to around 4,000 BC and the earliest evidence appears in specific locations, from which it firstly arose, and diffused outward over time to infect nearly every corner of the globe.
>
> A massive climate change shook the ancient world, when approximately 6,000 years ago vast areas of lush grassland and forest in the Old World began to quickly dry out and convert into harsh desert. The vast Sahara Desert, Arabian Desert, and the giant deserts of the Middle East and Central Asia simply did not exist prior to c. 4000 BC.

The need to survive by intensifying male aggression into violence and plunder is easy to explain, not only in terms of massive hunger but also in terms of the subordination of women (whom we may collectively view as the empathic voice of maternal tenderness); insensitivity to children; and even the ascetic characteristic of the civilized world — which, in turning against the Inner Child in each person, has turned against instinctual drives. For, as DeMeo observes:

> Famine and starvation is a severe trauma from which survivors rarely escape unscathed. A lot of people die, families are split apart, and babies and children are often abandoned, and suffer enormously. Starvation affects surviving children in an emotionally severe manner. They shrink from the exhausting heat and thirst, emotionally withdraw from the painful world, and simultaneously suffer a severe stunting of the entire brain and nervous system due to protein-calorie malnutrition. Even if such starved children later get all the food and water they want, they are deeply scarred in an emotional-neurological manner which forever changes their behavior — specifically, there is an implanted inhibition of any impulse of a pleasure-seeking, outward-reaching nature, and a discomfort with deeper forms of body-pleasure, in both maternal-infant or male-female expressions. Additionally, the child's view of the mother, who could not protect or feed the child during the famine period, is thereafter colored with suspicion and anger. These attitudes and behaviors are deeply protoplasmic in nature, and are passed on to ensuing generations no matter what the climate, by social institutions which reflect the character structure of the average individual at any given period of time.[6]

The observations of David W. Anthony complement those of DeMeo. In his recent book,[7] *The Horse, the Wheel and Language: How Bronze Age Riders from the Eurasian Steppes Shaped the Modern World*, Anthony shows how the spread of Indo-European languages in Europe and Asia followed the pattern of a patriarchal form of social organization that came into being in the Russian steppes north of the Caucasus, with the domestication of animals and the rise of metallurgy. He also shows that, contrary to the earlier assumption that the initial spread of the Proto-Indo-European dialects was a reflection of violent invasions, patriarchy was established more gradually, at a time of food scarcity, through the use of technology and commercial treaties imposed through terror.

But I do not need to present my readers with an erudite review of what is known of the history of patriarchy to convey my essential premise that the *great problem of civilization is none other than civilization itself.* Let me, rather, proceed to the contention that *civilization is not only the patriarchal organization of society, but also a patriarchal organization of the mind.* As later chapters will reveal, my emphasis is on the notion that *our present crisis is nothing other than an expression of the destructive, and increasingly unsustainable, obsolescence of the imbalance that patriarchy introduced among the father, the mother, and the child – in the family, in the realm of cultural values, and especially within the human mind.*

I am convinced that many of the grave problems now threatening our very survival by rendering our present form of life unsustainable are like the many heads of the great patriarchal *Beast*, and that it is high time we attend to our fundamental problem, beyond merely addressing its symptoms.

This view implies that our understanding of the tyranny of the father over the mother and the children throughout history should not be viewed as just one more facet of civilized consciousness, among others. Rather, we need to regard it as the common root of servitude; the disruption of fraternal bonds; violence; greed; self-antagonism; and other characteristics of our collective neurosis.

It would seem that when men took control of collective affairs, our minds — the *internal* counterpart of society — became unbalanced. While cooperation and competitiveness are in our psyche like two hands meant to operate in balance, cooperation (the feminine mode) became eclipsed in our social life by the masculine emphasis on competition. Today, competition is the very motor of our inhuman and depredatory economy.

The same can be said regarding tenderness and aggression. In each of us there is a severe self and a compassionate self; and it is appropriate to be affectionate or bellicose, depending on the moment and the circumstances. But instead of being free to employ both of our psychological "arms" according to what may fit the circumstances, history clearly shows that we have become on the whole too prone to violence, and underdeveloped in our capacity for compassion. (This is why it is timely that the Dalai Lama travels worldwide giving talks about how important a good heart is for the future of humanity, and not only for our personal development.)

Just as, in the dawn of civilization, patriarchal aggression eclipsed our empathetic sensitivity, favoring competitiveness over cooperation, so something equivalent took place regarding the similar complementarity of cultivation and exploitation. And we may say that the subordination, or eclipse, of the intra-psychic femininity — our "Inner Mother" — which is part of our healthy and wholesome mind has led us (along with the imbalance between cultivation and exploitation) to an alarming and ever-increasing ecocide.

On a *collective* scale, male power has taken over the political decisions of the civilized world throughout history, turning history into the expression of a hegemonic, violent, conquering, and possessive spirit.

On a *family* scale, patriarchal society is characterized by the institution of the *paterfamilias*, who — through his authority — takes possession and dominates over both wife and children. And just as the oppression of women results in the eclipse of love, so the oppression of children (in the outer world, as in the inner) has resulted in the eclipse of eros. It is precisely this antagonism between civilization as we have known it, on the one hand, and instinct and "the pleasure principle," on the other, that Freud emphasized in *Civilization and Its Discontents*.

Just as both the eclipse of love and the vilification of eros are intrinsic to the patriarchal mind, and thus lie at the heart of civilized life, so both the restoration of people's ability to love and the decriminalization of pleasure have been among the tasks of modern psychotherapy. It would be naive to expect psychotherapy alone to heal a sick society, and yet it cannot be denied that patriarchy has constituted an ever-present obstacle to mental health and inner balance. We may regard it as the basis of a universal neurosis that — contagiously propagating from generation to generation like a plague — carries it forward in time, like a plant propagating its genetic material.

In subtitling this chapter "Its Silenced Root," I wanted not only to draw attention to how the acknowledgment of the patriarchal spirit at the center of our *problematique* has been rejected, silenced, and denied, but also to suggest that — just as individual neurosis entails a narrowing of understanding (sustained by the operation of different "defense mechanisms") — so, on a collective level, the patriarchal spirit is defended by an active ignorance. For as Marcuse and Foucault have pointed out, it is not enough for something to be true in order for its truth to be recognized in academic circles or in the sphere of public opinion, where what is accepted as truth is also a function of vested interests, conformity, blindness, and the will of those in power. And without going into a detailed analysis of various resistances to the idea that the patriarchal mind is inherent in all known civilizations, I simply wish to note that social scientists have shared a common bias of looking down on matristic cultures (such as that of the Trobrianders, as well as the Iroquois and other American Indians) as "barbaric." And they still look down disapprovingly upon those who are interested in the matristic past of our history.

Yet I hope that a day of "revelation" may not be far off, when the fact of the patriarchal despotism underlying our seemingly free modern world may become obvious, along with the beastly destructiveness hidden under its loudly proclaimed democratic values.

CHAPTER 2

TÓTILA ALBERT
AND HIS VISION
OF A TRI-UNE SOCIETY

To confront the big picture seems like an overpowering challenge.

— Amartya Sen

THE IDEA THAT PATRIARCHY constitutes the world's meta-problem has become increasingly familiar to us over the years. As early as the 1980s, Fritjof Capra's book, *The Turning Point*, pointed out that "the first and perhaps most profound transition [of recent times] is due to the slow and reluctant but inevitable decline of patriarchy."[1] Shortly afterwards, Riane Eisler's book, *The Chalice and the Blade*,[2] made a decisive contribution by bringing public awareness to the idea that patriarchal society is not only unfair to women, but is also a burden for all humankind; and others such as David Korten (whose recent book is subtitled *From Empire to Earth Community*)[3] have integrated this perspective into their analysis of the present-day "Empire."

As mentioned in the previous chapter, however, it is to Johan J. Bachofen[4] that we owe the discovery of the patriarchal condition of our society. For his unearthing of an archaic "mother-rule" in the history of the Mediterranean peoples made it clear that — contrary to the belief up until that time — the patriarchal order had not characterized the whole of our history, and could thus not be said to be intrinsic to human nature. Up until his discovery, the prevailing conviction (still believed, even today, by the staunchest defenders of the status quo) was that "there have been wars since there are men."

Yet since then, we have begun to realize that there is neither love nor wisdom in attributing to our species a genetically determined and barbaric "lack of humanity." Thanks to the progress of archaeology as well as the contributions of archaeology and the reflections of Briffault, Gimbutas, DeMeo, and others, today it seems clear that wars and slavery have not always been with us, but began at a given time in history: during the late Neolithic or Chalcolithic times, when matristic culture gave way to the patriarchal regime.

Curiously, Bachofen never became a critic of patriarchy. On the contrary, he implicitly praised the advent of the "solar stage" in the development of human consciousness. This may well be the result of his being in tune with the culture of his time, particularly since many have failed to grasp the degradation of consciousness and the psycho-social pathology that went hand-in-hand with the alliance then established between technological progress and political power. Even in our own day, this view persists: for example, Ken Wilber has been applauded for contending that not only was the dawn of civilization the beginning of a glorious evolutionary rise, but also that the "The Fall of Man" has been nothing but a myth.

Nonetheless, Bachofen stimulated a profound cultural revolution, without ever seeking to do so. For one thing, he influenced Friedrich Engels, whose own interpretation of Bachofen's findings was expressed in his book, *Origins of the Family, Private Property and the State*. For another, Bachofen's findings provided an unparalleled stimulus for the rise of ethnology: his interpretation of prehistory roused pioneering field anthropologists to investigate the possible persistence of living matriarchal societies. He may even have had an indirect influence in shaping the American democratic dream. Founding fathers such as Thomas Jefferson and Benjamin Franklin — who had read Bachofen-enthusiast Lewis Henry Morgan,[5] and were personally acquainted with the matristic Iroquois — also came to respect Native Americans and their unheard-of democratic ways. Bachofen may even be seen, indirectly and yet decisively, as an invisible influence on the feminist movement that challenged the patriarchal spirit from the viewpoint of women's rights.

However, many years would pass before feminists, and the world in general, began to discover that patriarchy is not only an issue concerning justice between the sexes but also a disease that affects us all. Thus, when Eisler's *The Chalice and the Blade* first came out, the anthropologist Ashley Montagu saw fit to write that it "deserves to be considered the most important work since Darwin's *The Origin of Species*." Despite the fact that Eisler disclosed what had already been published in the scientific journals, Montagu's opinion is not only understandable, but also fair. For beyond merely bringing this information together, Eisler also gave voice to the idea that the *patriarchal organization of society constitutes the meta-problem of the world*. Yet although she contributed more than anyone towards creating a generalized awareness of this important idea, it is clear that she (like Capra before her) simply formulated something that was already "in the air."

The first to propose that the patriarchal organization of society constitutes our most fundamental illness was Tótila Albert, just as Bachofen was the indisputable discoverer of the matristic world. And I suspect that the ferment of Albert's thinking — which seeped into the California culture almost invisibly, through my own talks on this subject in the USA over the past thirty years — influenced people to reflect explicitly on something that was patently obvious, although never directly mentioned — much like the famed emperor's nudity in Hans Christian Andersen's tale, "The Emperor's New Clothes."

Though I have written about Tótila Albert in two of my previous books, *The End of Patriarchy* and *Songs of Enlightenment*, let me briefly introduce him to you here. He was born in Chile in 1892 of German parents, and died there in 1967. He received his higher education in Berlin, and became a very well-known sculptor there following World War I. After productive and successful years there, where he was sometimes regarded as "the German Rodin," the death of his father precipitated in him a profound experience that constituted the beginning of an "inner journey," one which turned him into both a mystic and a poet.

While still in Germany in the 1930s, he wrote an epic poem entitled "The Birth of the Self." Afterwards, his well-tuned ear seemed to open to the inner dimension of Beethoven's music, and he set forth to decode Beethoven's works in chronological sequence so as to reconstitute the great composer's psycho-spiritual development. Unfortunately, this project was interrupted by the onset of World War II, and he returned to Chile, where the need to make a living constrained him to return to sculpture. But the process of spiritual awakening that made him into a poet, one with the gift of musical hermeneutics, also gave him an understanding of the human condition, and a wish to shake those with whom he came in contact out of their complacent acceptance of "patriarchal ways." And though he never undertook the writing of social criticism or social philosophy, this predilection gave him the vocation of a prophet who wanted to contribute to the transformation of the world.

However, he was one of those prophets who went unheeded in his own land and time. His living heritage only passed into the future though Dr. Lola Hoffman (a Jungian psychotherapist who, in turn, influenced Humberto Maturana) and myself. Thus far, his influence has manifested implicitly, in me and in my approach to transformational work with groups, and (in recent years) explicitly, in my efforts to transmit his ideas more directly.

Tótila died in Santiago in September 1967. He is remembered in his country of birth as a sculptor, through his various monuments. Nobody is aware that he was the first to directly denounce patriarchy as the fundamental problem of the world, and also the first explicit adversary of patriarchal society. Tótila dreamed of a social transformation in which patriarchal hegemony could be replaced by a balance among father, mother, and child — both in the social family and within the intra-psychic family: that is, within each individual's mind.

While feminism has either competed with patriarchal values or imagined an alternative society where tribal and ecological values would prevail, Tótila Albert emphasized the *inner*, or psycho-spiritual, way of transcending the patriarchal condition. He understood that only through psychologically healthy individuals whose minds and lives operate as an "embrace of three" (the Inner Father, Mother, and Child components) could a healthy society arise. We might say that through his emphasis on a politics of individual transformation, he was a forerunner of a view that we have come to associate with the New Age. As for traditional religions, he criticized them for colluding with the patriarchal mind by failing to take issue with the institution of the *paterfamilias*, as well as for their conformity and for their adoption of the institutionalized authoritarianism of political life.

Tótila used the German expression "*Das Dreimal Unser*" in reference to his vision of a healthy society, and translated this expression into Spanish as "*El Tres Veces Nuestro*" — in English, literally as "Our Three." Yet I think that this expression might be better rendered as "The World of the Three," perhaps even "The *Kingdom* of Three." This would emphasize the continuity of his vision with that of those who spoke of the *Kingdom of God*, and also underscore the sacredness of the three inner persons, which he understood as the echo of cosmic principles.

In implicit reference to "Our Father" (the opening of Christianity's fundamental prayer), Tótila's expression "Our Three" implies an alternative to the one-sidedly patriarchal interpretation of the Divine, and also to the one-sided exaltation of the father over the mother and the child in the human world. Offering an alternative to the patriarchal world, he used the expression to mean a future era characterized by the balance of the inner and outer "three" — a balance that he saw as the only alternative to global catastrophe. Such an alternative to an ever-increasingly dysfunctional and obsolete patriarchy would, of course, encourage people's natural sense of communion with life and the living, including an appreciation for the sacredness of the Earth and of motherhood, and would enable them to develop spontaneously a sense of their own inner Divine Child as well as an awareness of their condition as "children of heaven and earth."

Because the inner trinity envisioned by Tótila Albert was closely associated with (but not identical to) the trinity of intellect, emotion, and action — which characterize the three components of our brain, as indicated by Gurdjieff — we might consider the three inner persons whose disunity he lamented as the phenomenological counterpart of a lack of integration within these parts of our "tri-une brain." Thus it may be said that both Tótila Albert and Gurdjieff shared the same vision of human fulfillment — and of human wretchedness. Yet Tótila only came to know of Gurdjieff through me, long after he had formulated his "message of the three," which had arisen simply as an echo of the experience of integration that took place in him in the aftermath of his father's death.

Since Tótila conceived of fullness and health as a three-fold inner embrace among these inner persons within the individual, and rather implicitly acknowledged the relationship between such inner persons and different aspects of love, it was natural for me to take a special interest in viewing these subpersonalities in the human mind from the perspective of love. Before I explain my interpretation of mental health and self-realization as a three-fold embrace among *eros*, *agape*, and *philia*, however, it is fitting to say something more about Tótila Albert, to whom I owe the trinitarian anthropology that has inspired my psycho-social understanding, my educational work with groups, and the present book.

I had the good fortune of becoming Tótila Albert's closest friend in Chile, the land where he was born (as I was) and to which he later returned after years of rich creative activity and deep transformation in Berlin during the 1920s and '30s. I imagine that my musical compositions contributed to his taking an interest in me at that time (although they later came to seem an idle luxury to me); but I think that our friendship was also stimulated by the fact that he was an unrecognized prophet in his own land and I, perceiving his wisdom and his light, little by little became his apprentice and companion.

Tótila had the appearance of a patriarch. His noble features — along with his somewhat Einsteinian long hair — were well known by Chileans in his day, among whom he was famous as the sculptor who had produced various monuments in the city. There was something about him — perhaps the combination of an expression that conveyed spiritual maturity, along with his pained concern for the state of the world — that I associated with the prophet Jeremiah, although later I came to associate his personality mostly with that of Elijah.

He was usually known and addressed by his first name — Tótila — and I think this said something about his warm and informal way of being, which invited intimacy. Later, I would know a comparable case in Fritz Perls, the originator of Gestalt Therapy, whose wish to be called "Fritz" rather than "Dr. Friedrich Perls" (as certain later Gestaltists have preferred) constituted a counter-cultural and anti-authoritarian gesture. Congruent with this counter-patriarchal spirit was that he engaged with me in a brotherly, rather than a fatherly, attitude, despite the age difference that could well have made him my grandfather.

Though I strongly associate the content of Tótila's influence on my life with the influence that Gurdjieff had on me when I read *Beelzebub*[6] and the works of Ouspensky, their styles could not have been more different. For while Gurdjieff (much like Beelzebub) was severe, Tótila was warm and friendly. Also, while Gurdjieff was ironic and disdainful, Tótila was tragic in his suffering for the world.

It was providential that these two extraordinary influences coincided in the same period of my life — the beginning of my university years — and most fortunate that the nearness of a living self-realized being reinforced in me the indirect presence of the more remote master, Gurdjieff, who had already inspired me to feel that beings of a kind I had never before imagined existed in the world. Just as the authoritativeness radiating from Gurdjieff, even through his written words, lent additional validity to Tótila — a teacher who never "taught" (in the sense that he never adopted an authority role) — so my closeness with Tótila brought me closer to the things that Gurdjieff, that mysterious initiate of a Central Asian esoterism, explained to Ouspensky and others in Russia at the turn of the twentieth century. Tótila and Gurdjieff especially coincided in their tri-une vision, although Gurdjieff formulated it more abstractly in terms of an "affirmative force," a "negative force," and a "neutralizing force" that entered into play in all things, whereas Tótila preferred the biological vocabulary of father-mother-child.

Yet where Gurdjieff took the role of a guide who led and encouraged his disciples in an effort to transcend the limits of their personalities, it seemed to me that Tótila was more like a bard who sang "from the other shore." Using the language of Castaneda, I would say that he was a "benefactor" to me rather than a teacher or guru. Yet my knowledge of Gurdjieff made me wish early on that I, too, might have a teacher. And so it was that, in a quest for a practical guidance to transformation, I later came to meet Fritz Perls, Idries Shah, Oscar Ichazo, Suleiman Dede, Swami Muktananda, Tarthang Tulku, and others.

Many years would pass before I could come to understand Tótila through my personal ripening. However, I feel great satisfaction in the realization that the responsibility I have undertaken as a bearer of his legacy has not only stimulated my own growth, but that this growth, in turn, is also finally allowing me to serve as a bridge to the message of my prophetic friend. Although he failed to be understood by his contemporaries, at this time he may well contribute to that change in direction of the course of history on which our future depends.

CHAPTER 3

CIVILIZATION AS HUBRIS

This central reality of the West is marvelously expressed in the old Latin phrase: *Corruptio optimi quae est pessima* [the corruption of the best is the worst]...

I want to speak of the mysterious darkness that envelops our world, the demonic night paradoxically resulting from the world's equally mysterious vocation to glory.

My subject is a mystery of faith, a mystery whose depth of evil could not have come to be without a corresponding and contrary height in the history of salvation.

— Ivan Illich, "Hospitality and Pain"

THE IDEA THAT UNDERSTANDING the past can help us understand the present has inspired the most interesting historians, from Herodotus on to modern times. When we expand this idea to apply to the development of individuals, we can learn much by looking for correspondences between the healthy development of individuals and the development of a mature society. Just as in the individual therapeutic process, where the person needs to understand the origins of personal pain and dysfunction in order to transcend them, so at the social level we also may need to understand the origins of the patriarchal condition in order to overcome it.

Just as we often forget our own early history in infancy, as individuals, so as a human culture have we forgotten our collective prehistory — nor are we likely to find any remnants of ruins that will bring it back to life. Unless the bare, isolated facts uncovered by archaeology and mythology are enough to satisfy our thirst for knowledge, we will insist on formulating a vision. And this means that we need to set about interpreting the incomplete data we have.

This, then, is my rationale for presenting, in this chapter, conjectures and interpretations based on incomplete evidence — evidence that may well be impossible to prove. However, since we do need to understand, and since we cannot know what really happened five or six millennia ago, we must therefore imagine. After all, some archaeologists today look approvingly upon the reconstructions of our prehistory proposed by some novelists who have written of the upper Paleolithic era or of the Celts. And so I shall attempt to imagine the origin of patriarchal society, based on more information than that which was available to Tótila Albert when he gave the matter the full scope of his mind and heart.

Women, it is believed, invented agriculture. Since planting and harvesting seem originally to have been woman's domain, it is understandable that these activities and knowledge would have given women economic power during the time when humans shifted from a nomadic lifestyle to a sedentary one. And we can easily imagine that with such economic power — along with the voice of the community (for the bonds among women seem to have knit the sedentary world closely together) — the feminine mind had an exceptional opportunity to influence the culture.

It is my impression that during the period of cultural flourishing of the early Neolithic, mythical heroes — semi-divine beings, in a certain sense — made their entrance on the scene in the late Neolithic era or during that mythical "Bronze Age" that preceded the urban revolution, inculcating in their contemporaries an aspiration for the superhuman. However, this great respect for the superhuman came hand-in-hand with a desacralization of the merely human — of the natural world and of animal nature. Thus, at the same time that we progressed, we also degenerated. In this way, the superhuman stature of our "civilizers" made us not only greater, but also grandiose — and, therefore, smaller.

Many different things have been said about the rise of patriarchal civilization after the matristic era, about six thousand years ago in the "Fertile Crescent." For example, we know that the invention of irrigation introduced a new stage in the intensification of agriculture — not only because it was now possible to cultivate crops on a scale that could feed a much larger population, but also because it was now men who worked in the fields. Their greater physical strength, which gave them an advantage in plowing the land, may have been the beginning of the transfer of economic power from women to men in the late Neolithic era.

Women's economic power had favored the development of the maternal spirit in the culture, endowing its inhabitants with greater care in their relationships with each other and the earth. And it is likely that the transfer of this power to men not only helped them gain dominance, but also caused the masculine spirit — which was oriented toward the *transcendence* of the natural order — to prevail. This obviously had its benefits: over time it would lead to the development of astronomy and writing, among other advances, and would deepen the intuition of a cosmic celestial order, as revealed through the movement of the planets and stars. Yet it would seem that the development of proto-science, which surely was favorable to survival from its inception, apparently was soon recruited in the service of masculine power and dominance.

The birth of civilization as we know it seems mysterious. Explaining it as solely a response to such factors as the challenge of climatic changes, the need to organize the community, and the surplus of agricultural production (which so much secular academic writing has concentrated on) seems insufficient. Rather, it is as if each civilization emerged from some kind of spiritual inspiration, and manifested in full splendor from the time of its earliest period.

Ever since Plato, some have thought that the Egyptian and Aegean civilizations inherited a legacy from a prior and lost civilization. In the case of Egypt in particular, it is difficult to explain how such a high civilization — with its astronomy, its medicine, and its technology of construction — could have risen as it did without any apparent prior evolution. Moreover, signs of water erosion on the Sphinx suggest that it may have existed for millennia *before* the great pyramids. Some have thought that the influence on the Egyptians came from lost Atlantis.

In South America, too, the Mayans and the civilization of Tiahuanacu, near Lake Titicaca in Bolivia, pose a riddle. The pyramid Akapana, with its extremely advanced stone-modeling techniques, still puzzles scientists. As for the monumental Peruvian fortress of Sacsahuaman, usually attributed to the Incas, it is impossible to imagine how it could have been constructed during the short life-span of the Inca empire (about a hundred years) and before the arrival of the Spaniards: it is made of stones weighing more than two hundred tons, which were brought from distant quarries by inconceivable means and carved in an extremely precise and complex fashion before being fitted into the huge walls. One cannot help suspecting the existence of a technology that, even today, seems so advanced that it has prompted some to believe in the intervention of extraterrestrials. Yet is this bizarre-sounding idea really any different from what the Greeks thought, when they imagined a "heroic era" in which demigods lived among humans?

Vestiges of the legendary Atlantis have yet to be found, though there is always the possibility that evidence of an ancient civilization may turn up in the still-unexplored region of the sunken delta of the antediluvian, pre-Sumerian Mesopotamia or in the Indian Ocean. Yet aside from this possibility, one can imagine that at the dawn of civilization, certain beings were possessed by a "divine spirit," demonstrating a level of consciousness that made them appear to their contemporaries as living gods — a combination of extraterrestrial and supernatural.

This is why the legends that ascribe the origin of civilization to certain "civilizers," such as Osiris or Quetzalcoatl, seem credible. Could such cultures have arisen from a contagion of consciousness spread by individuals manifesting a divine inspiration not yet known by prehistoric shamans? An inspiration seeming to come from "celestial gods," as they have been called, in contrast with that of the more earth-bound "chthonic gods"? From a transcendent and masculine god, in contrast with the mother-like and immanent divinity of nature?

Whatever the answer to this, it is difficult to doubt that humans venerated motherhood as early as Paleolithic times, and that in the Neolithic era Europeans associated the myth of the Great Goddess with the mystery of the resurrection — symbolized by the apparent death of nature in winter and the return of life in spring, as well as by the lunar cycle. We may ask, then: If the mystery of the great journey of the soul (on its path to the supreme state) was already known during the matristic era, what *else* did those heroes who went down in history as the sons or messengers of celestial gods discover?

I suspect that their unprecedented glory may not have been a reflection of a more elevated consciousness at all, but rather the combination of pre-scientific knowledge and an ignorant excitement, as the Sufi saint and Afghan chieftain Jan Fishan Khan,[1] an ancestor of Idries Shah, expressed to the British authorities:

> My great-great grandfather, Sayed Jan-Fishan Khan, was invited to India and a great military display was put on for him.
>
> It was intended to illustrate to this independent Afghan chief that the warlike capacities of the British Empire were such that it would be to his advantage to respect it.
>
> An artillery officer was attached to the Khan at one point, and he shouted enthusiastically, drawing the chief's attention every time the shells hit their target.

This man and several others were subsequently invited back to Paghman, to be the guests of Jan-Fishan Khan.

As they were sitting at the banquet a man came up to Jan-Fishan Khan and said something. As soon as he had answered him, Jan-Fishan turned to the British officers and said, apparently in excitement: "Did you hear that?"

"What did he say?" they asked.

"It is not 'what did he say,' said the Khan, "but the fact that I understood him and he understood me!"

The officers were nonplussed.

The following day, Jan-Fishan Khan took his guests on a tour of his stables. He pointed out some horses.

One of the horses was being fed. "Look, how he eats!" roared the Khan.

Another was being exercised. "He can actually walk, and run!" the Khan exulted, clapping his hands.

The visitors thought that their host must be mad.

They were unable to fathom his extraordinary behavior until he had to say, as they were leaving: "You have seen, gentlemen, if you have guns which do exactly what they were designed to do — hitting the target — I, too, am surrounded by things which also appear to be fulfilling their function quite adequately. What I have learned from you is to get excited about it."

The phenomenon called "inflation," described by Jung, has long been known in spiritual traditions as an apprentice's exaltation — a "holy madness" that is a prelude to "contraction" or the equivalent of a descent into hell that supervenes before true spiritual maturity is achieved.

In the 1980s, I was invited by the Graduate Theological Union in Berkeley, California to participate in a study group, which eventually turned into a conference about conversion and coercion in the new religions and sects that had emerged during the 1970s and '80s. There, I spoke about how — given the freedoms of the modern world, and the intensification of the seeking spirit that followed the crisis of traditional ideology — it was not uncommon for people (mostly in the therapeutic community) who had not followed a monastic discipline or even an explicitly spiritual path to show signs of the "sorcerer's apprentice syndrome"; and that it was precisely in this narcissistic grandiosity that one could find the origin of the new sects that were then provoking such antagonism among the followers of the traditional religions.

The history of religion gives us abundant examples of how the "spiritual journey" goes through a phase of expansion and then contraction before bringing the wayfarer to his or her destination. These phases appear not only in parables and myths (such as that of Osiris, the civilizing king who later descended into the kingdom of the dead), but also through the lives of the mystics. Each of these phases involves a pathology; and the explanation (as I have shown in my book, *Songs of Enlightenment: The Tale of the Hero in the Evolution of Western Poetry*[2]) may be found in the fact that when the higher life of the mind is born — i.e., the ability for contemplative experience — the "small mind" (with its neuroses) still persists, and feels alternately stimulated and depressed. Inflation, then, is something like the exaltation of the personality when in close contact with something that transcends it — just as the "night" following it, so well described by St. John of the Cross, consists of a corresponding devaluation of the personality in the face of spiritual intuition.

I am therefore proposing that not only the "new sects" but also the classical religions have originated within the grandiose inflation of immature enlightenment. For clearly, sectarianism is by no means a recent phenomenon. It is only one that has become invisible through its universality (although it has been apparent through religious wars and the systemic antagonism toward rival new sects). My contention is that — like civilization itself — the sectarian nature of traditional religiosity is derived from an archaic and grandiose inflation or exaltation.

Two contradictory facts converge to prove this: one, the undeniable spiritual inspiration of civilizations; and two, the unquestionable criminality of many religions throughout history (or, stated slightly differently, the use of religion to rationalize violence). This apparent contradiction echoes an analogous phenomenon that takes place on an individual scale: *mystical experience is a light that may cast a long shadow.*

If we wish to understand how civilizations were born through the experience of the sacred, we would do well to examine the different interpretations of the sacred that have been expressed in mythology and art since prehistoric times.

It seems that humankind's original religion had the Mother Goddess as its focal point. This can be seen in the remarkable female statuettes and impressive representations of the Goddess found at the entrance to caves, which were thought to have been places of ritual associated with the womb of Mother Nature.

Since remote antiquity, the Goddess seems to have personified both nature and more than nature, something transcending the visible world as well. Through Her association with the moon, with its monthly cycle of expansion and contraction, She seemed to reflect not just the menstrual cycle and the cycle of seasonal regeneration of the plant world, but also the mystery of permanence beyond transformation: that is, beyond the cycle of life and death. The moon, like the plant world, periodically disappears from the sky and reappears. In its waning, waxing, and full phases, which came to symbolize the "triple goddess" (one with a virginal face, another with the face of a woman in the prime of life, and a third with the face of an old woman), we find the most ancient formulation of trinity in the history of religion. This moon cycle also includes a dark or invisible phase, however; and this we may take to be a "visible" expression of invisibility: a symbolic expression of something transcending the manifest life cycle. It is not true to say, then, that the intuition of the Cosmic Mother was simply a personification of visible life. It is truer to say that life itself was conceived as only partly visible, nature being perceived as intrinsically mysterious.

In the early Neolithic, the Goddess clearly was also associated with bovine animals — undoubtedly, in part, because of the moonlike shape of their horns, but mainly because of their milk and even their flesh. For surely they were perceived as being in the world to feed us, not only with their generous udders but also through the sacrifice of their bodies. And while the temples at the centers of the early cities, at the dawn of the "urban revolution" of patriarchy, were dedicated to celestial gods, the earlier Mesopotamian temples (also at the center of their respective villages) contained sacred cows.

But by the late Neolithic era, the eternal and mutable aspects of the Goddess already had become polarized. The conception of two deities arose: one, the Great Goddess, who retained the association with indestructible life beyond her manifestations; and the other her consort, symbolized by the bull, alluding to the individual who dies-and-is-reborn. And thus emerged the formula for the myth of the hero — a man who becomes divine through death and resurrection.

Tammuz, Adonis, Dionysius, Osiris — all are the same hero with different names (as Sir James George Frazer[3] showed), and are emblematic expressions of the process of transformation that lies within the power of each individual (according to the famous interpretation of Joseph Campbell[4]).

Such, it seems, was the mythological prelude to civilization — a form of hierarchical organization of society, in which authority shifted from the human community to divine command, embodied in the person of the priest-king. This mythological vision may have persisted into the time of the ancient Mesopotamian city-states in Uruk, Ur, Lagash, and others, where the vulva-shaped temples dedicated to the Great Mother Goddess were first replaced by altars.

Yet it would seem that patriarchal civilization proper did not arise with these first cities, as V. Gordon Childe proposed with his concept of the "urban revolution," but somewhat later: when the powerful officiants, who had become even more powerful, turned themselves into gods; and when the king, rather than the Goddess, was worshipped as the mystery of death-that-gives-life.

At first, it seems, it was the wise and saintly priests who anointed and guided the kings; but in time the kings seized supreme authority (as well as control over their death, as Frazer so masterfully showed in his erudite twelve volumes of *The Golden Bough*).

Although Freud proposed that the archaic sacrificial practice of the kings was nothing more than the social expression of the rebellion of sons against their fathers — who, on becoming old, could no longer defend their autocratic government against brute force, similarly to that which occurs in groups of gorillas — I find Joseph Campbell's explanations more plausible. He relies for his understanding on a concept borrowed from Thomas Mann, which Campbell calls "mythic inflation."

Firstly, though, I should explain what Campbell, in his book *Eastern Mythology*, calls "mythic *identification*" — referring to the time when the ancient kings became one with the divine through a sacrificial rite.

We may imagine that by embracing death, the ancient kings identified with the divinity and thus expected eternal life. Yet although modern scholars have viewed the self-immolation of kings as not only superstitious but also barbaric, I imagine that those who died through sacrifice (as their tombs show) served, at the dawn of civilization, as an insurance or guarantee instituted by the priests against the possible abuse of power.

Few people in our day and age have known the experience of cosmic consciousness. And yet it is possible that at that time, the consciousness of a king who was willing to sacrifice himself might have evolved to the point of a mystical communion with the eternal. We may also suspect that the wise priests (who created the monarchic institution, while remaining close advisors to its leaders) may have designed such ritual sacrifice as a wise way of regulating the access to power, in view of the danger of its perpetuation. For they knew that only the enlightened, by virtue of realizing their supreme identity, could be detached enough to accept the condition of a terminal sacrifice.

It is clear that the first kings, in their desire to embody the myth of the god-who-dies-and-is-reborn, were willing to immolate themselves when the right moment had arrived (according to the priests' observations of the movement of the stars and the arrival of the ideal cosmic coordinates). However, we also know that this institution of embodied sacrifice was later transformed, in Egypt and Sumer, into a *symbolic* ritual. However, the practice of physical sacrifice continued elsewhere, even into recent times, as has been amply shown by Leo Frobenius in his *African Archives*. Among the Shilluk people of Sudan, Frobenius writes, "the priests, who were the only ones who knew the will of God (whom they called Nayakang), made sure the king died after seven years or, if the harvest failed or the animals did badly, even sooner."[5] Campbell quotes Duarte Barbosa, who described the coast of West Africa and Malabar at the beginning of the sixteenth century:

> The most vivid example on record of an "immolation" of the sacred king is probably that in Duarte Barbosa's *Description of the Coasts of East Africa and Malabar in the Beginning of the Sixteenth Century*. The god-king of the south Indian province of Quilacare in Malabar (an area having a strongly matriarchal tradition to this day) had to sacrifice himself at the end of the length of time required by the planet Jupiter for a circuit of the zodiac and return to its moment of retrograde motion in the sign of Cancer — which is to say, twelve years. When his time came, the king had a wooden scaffolding constructed and spread over with hangings of silk. And when he had ritually bathed in a tank, with great ceremonies and to the sound of music, he proceeded to the temple, where he paid worship to the divinity. Then he mounted the scaffolding and, before the people, took some very sharp knives and began to cut off parts of his body — nose, ears, lips, and all his members, and as much of his flesh as he was able — throwing them away and round about, until so much of his blood was spilled that he began to faint, whereupon he slit his throat.[6]

The most impressive aspect of this testimony is the celebratory nature of the ritual. The king seems willing to offer his flesh and blood in the same spirit as cutting flowers or plucking fruits to deposit on an altar. For by shedding his vestments of flesh, this officiant has full confidence that this ritual will lead him to the culmination of his destiny: eternal consciousness.

During the early period of masculine rule, it would seem that the kings were still under the control of the mystics, who constituted the true and hidden authority of the society. But the moment came when these kings would set themselves up as the supreme power.

Matters were different in Egypt and Sumer. In Sumer, the kings adopted a more modest role as representatives of the divine. In Egypt, they not only maintained their identity as gods but also proclaimed their supreme divinity as the source of the blessings of all the other gods. In both cases, however, the kings began to practice a merely symbolic self-sacrifice. No longer did they enact the (originally Neolithic) once-fatal love-death ritual of the *hieros gamos* in their flesh and blood, but now they designated a *surrogate* to mate in a public ceremony with a priestess to guarantee the earth's fertility. I suspect they must have intuited that this trick managed to prolong only their life and power, and not their eternity; for in this way we can understand the parallel escalation in the magnitude of their authority and the multiplication of compensatory sacrifices. The pharaohs' attachment to their lives and their power, which led them to avoid their own deaths from the first dynasty onward, explains the longing for eternity that is so prominent in the funeral cult.

Just as Joseph Campbell writes about "mythic identification" in reference to the ancient situation in which the king experiences himself as one with the divinity, and is also seen that way by his subjects, Campbell also writes about "mythic *inflation*," referring to the psychological situation that followed.

> It is surely worth observing, that, although in the period of the great tombs of the pharaoh of Dynasty I those mighty bulls when departing drew with them into the underworld all of their numerous herds of cows... with their mythological role as should have required of them — mighty kings — a like submission to ritual death.[7]

Commenting that "through his identity with the bull god that impregnates the heavenly goddess Hathor, who has the shape of a cow," Campbell explains that during the first centuries of the *hieratic* city-states, kings gave their bodies for sacrifice or even performed self-immolation during a festival. However, the creators of the first *political* state no longer offered themselves but symbolically sacrificed bulls, pigs, sheep, or goats to the priestly guardians (who, in other times, had derived their knowledge of the "right order" — *maat* — by observing the celestial bodies). The sacrifice became merely a symbolic garment:

> Instead of that old, dark, terrible drama of the king's death... the audience now watched a solemn symbolic mime, the Sed festival, in which the king renewed his pharaonic warrant without submitting to the personal inconvenience of a literal death. The rite was celebrated, some authorities believe, according to a cycle of thirty years.... Others have it, however, that the only scheduling factor was the king's own desire and command. Either way, the real hero of the great occasion was no longer the timeless Pharaoh, who puts on pharaohs, like clothes, and puts them off, but the living garment of flesh and bone, this particular pharaoh So-and-so, who, instead of giving himself to the part, now had found a way to keep the part to himself. And this he did simply by stepping the mythological image

down one degree. Instead of Pharaoh changing pharaohs, it was the pharaoh who changed costumes.[8]

In this way, Campbell notes, the original ritual through which the old king transferred his power to the new king was transformed into an allegory in which the king's death was merely symbolic. However, those same kings demanded that when their death did arrive, in the end, they be accompanied into their tombs by their wives, their concubines, their guards, and their other servants.

This brings to mind the Hindu widow who (until only a few centuries ago) so identified with Sati — the mother goddess and consort of Siva — that she had total faith in the teaching proclaiming the profound oneness of individual consciousness with the transcendent cosmic consciousness, and thus did not resist self-immolation on the funeral pyre or tomb of her dead husband but rather experienced the ritual with full devotion. We may imagine that those who gave their lives to accompany the Sumerian kings to their tombs did the same.

But is it *possible* for an individual to come to eternal life through the love of others?

Although this idea has been celebrated in epic poems such as *Faust*, whose eponymous hero was saved in the nether world by Margaret, as Dante had been saved by Beatrice in the *Divine Comedy*[9] — and in spite of the idea of redemption through Christ's death, which is at the heart of St. Paul's formulation of Christianity — perhaps such narratives only amplify and symbolize the favorable effects of love on human development. The association between such thinking with an historic epoch, in which divinized men sacrificed their women and children (as well as their servants and even dogs) instead of taking the leap that their predecessors heroically took into the primordial nothingness, suggests something else. I propose that when those ancient kings began to sacrifice others instead of practicing the self-sacrifice through which their ancestors had identified with the divinity, they developed a growing fear of death, which even their increasing number of victims could not appease.

○

However, this still does not explain the transition from "mythic identification" to "mythic inflation," or the shift from faith to religious manipulation of the people. Yet the historical context of this transition is clear enough that we do not require an erudite investigation into forgotten events. In Anne Baring and Jules Cashford's excellent book, *The Myth of the Goddess: Evolution of an Image,* in the introduction to their chapter about Indo-European and Semitic peoples they comment that:

> We can only wonder how the goddess cultures of the Bronze Age would evolve had they not been disrupted by the arrival of migratory warrior tribesmen who imposed their mythology and their patriarchal customs on the agricultural people whose territory they invaded.[10]

These glorifiers of the warrior spirit, with their domesticated horses and their battle axes, invaded sedentary peoples from Europe to India during the latter part of the Bronze Age in the name of their celestial gods — lightning, thunder, fire, wind, and storms — and the impact of these invasions on these peoples was dramatic. Campbell writes that, especially at the beginning of the Bronze Age (1250 B.C. in the Levant):

> The old cosmology, and mythologies of the goddess mother were radically transformed, reinterpreted, and in large measure even suppressed by those suddenly intrusive patriarchal warrior

tribesmen displaced from their original lands by desertification, whose traditions have come down to us chiefly in the Old and New Testaments and in the myths of Greece.[11]

More specifically, he explains that both invading peoples introduced the idea of an opposition between the powers of light *and* darkness, imposing this polarity over the ancient vision in which the totality contains both light and darkness in an ever-changing relationship. Both mythologies — the Greek, and the Old and New Testaments — give evidence of a de-sacralization of the nature of human life, in contrast with the vision of Neolithic farmers, who lived closely with the earth and the rhythms of the immanent goddess — with life in its entirety.

It would seem that the descendants of the Paleolithic hunters and gatherers of the steppes just north of the Caspian and Black Seas were negatively influenced by the harsh conditions of their inhospitable environment. Not only did they turn into warriors, but they also turned into pessimists: they came to believe in an absolute separation between humans and the divinity. And their own influence, as Baring and Cashford point out, was just as negative: now the *goddesses* as well as the gods "are infected by warrior ethos, ratifying the barbaric actions of the kings whose territorial ambitions draw them ever more deeply into the compulsion to conquer and enslave other peoples."[12] The authors quote Eliade on the idea that now "the pursuit and killing of wild animals becomes the mythical model for the conquest of a territory and the founding of a state."[13]

For those who doubt the extent of the upheaval produced by these "barbarian invasions," as an explanation for the spiritual deterioration of a country as isolated and powerful as Egypt, I would like to explore further the vast cultural phenomenon that resulted from the triumph of the patriarchal peoples. This phenomenon is one that Campbell has described as "the Great Reversal,"[14] characterized as the origin of the differences between eastern and western religions. As Baring and Cashford write:

> As the Bronze Age progresses, a new thread enters the great tapestry of human evolution. It is terror: not the terror of nature, but the terror of death by the hand of other human beings. The lamentations that begin to appear during the third millennium B.C., rising to a crescendo during the second and first millennia B.C., bear witness to an ever-rising tide of barbarism, which battered the walls of the cities in the valleys and flowed over their inhabitants, bringing death and slavery to many thousands and mortal fear to all.... Enormous walls were built round every city, like the ones Gilgamesh built round Uruk in about 2700 B.C.... The new conditions required a ruler of superior strength and courage, a defender of his city with the limitless powers of emergency. With the rise of the powerful king, the epic came into being, celebrating the heroic exploits of the warrior-ruler. The destruction of city in war was experienced by the conquered people as the anger or hatred of a god, and likened to a hurricane-force wind.[15]

Apart from the fact that *leaders* of the old civilizations maintained close contact with each other (their mail system, it has been discovered, was comparable to our own), the following lament of an Egyptian man in dialogue with his soul reveals how the new situation was felt in this formerly strong and orderly country:

> To whom shall I speak today?
> Brothers are bad,
> the friends of today do not love.
>
> Hearts are greedy,
> everyone robs his neighbor's goods.

To whom shall I speak today?
Kindness has perished,
violence rules all.

The criminal is an intimate friend.
The brother with whom one dealt is a foe.

To whom shall I speak today?
Forgotten is the past.
Today one does not help him who helped.

Faces are blank.
Everyone turns his face from his brothers.

Death is in front of my face today,
like the clearing of the sky,
as when a man grasps what he did not know before.

Death is in front of my face today,
like a man's longing to see his home,
having spent many years in captivity.[16]

All this confirms the notion that a great catastrophe occurred in the Middle East and the Mediterranean after the
dawn of civilizations — a catastrophe that may be understood
as a result of that other catastrophe discussed in Chapter 1:
the desertification of the Saharasian belt, which originated the
"barbaric invasions." And we may imagine that those among
the "noble savages" of the Paleolithic Era who did not join in
the "agricultural revolution" (and who offered sacrifices in an
attempt to balance the natural order by imitating the generosity of nature) not only failed to turn into nicer people, but
on the contrary intensified their struggle for survival in their
rebellion against the incipient matristic culture, and for the
first time established charismatic masculine authority as an alternative to the authority of the tribe or community.

It is understandable that not only life but also religion
changed through the invasions of these nomadic predatory

warriors, in whom we can recognize the predecessors of the masters of our own culture. And we may find this shift reflected in mythology: for the first time, the Mother Goddess appears as evil, and the avenging god is seen as a hero-savior.

The new sensibility was first expressed in the Babylonian myth of Marduk, who destroys the feminine dragon, Tiamat, as a figure of the primordial creative chaos. However, this demonization of the feminine was not the only reflection of the "Great Reversal" in the religious life of the peoples. Ancient goddesses were also transformed into warriors, as in the case of Ishtar, who became the goddess of love and war in the Babylonian pantheon. Similarly, Athena, also a warrior, was born not of a woman but rather out of the head of Zeus, the father of the gods.

If we consider the conquest of ancient matristic cultures by the thunderous inhabitants of the steppes as a case of Hegelian dialectics, intrinsic to evolution (the *thesis* of matristic society and the *antithesis* of patriarchy), then we are still awaiting the felicitous *synthesis*. For while it is true that notable cultures emerged from the hybridization of conquerors and the conquered — from the India of the Upanishads to Buddhism, and even to Classical Greece — the historical phenomenon at issue seems primarily some kind of accident: a triumph of power over wisdom; a universal fall that, in early patriarchal society, involved the loss of the excellent human attributes and accomplishments of a noble past (as in the case of "the sacred citadel" of Troy).

Girard[17] has noted how ritual sacrifice — so central to the religions of classical civilizations — has arisen to sanctify violence. We can also see sacrifice as a ceremony designed to *validate* a fundamental act of patriarchy: a *sacred violence*, at the service of a supposedly divine order, on the part of those who believed they had a divine right to rule over less conscious beings. Gil Bailie, in his book, *Violence Unveiled*, writes:

> Caiphas invoked a mechanism for preserving culture as old as culture itself. It deals with the Assyria-Babylonian myth in which Marduk created the world by killing the monster Tiamat, or the Teutonic myth that narrates how Odin shaped the world by throwing Ymir's body from the sea made from his own blood, or the declaration of Pope Urban II that the First Crusade was the will of God, or Thomas Jefferson, who said that the tree of liberty must be refreshed from time to time with the blood of patriots and tyrants, or Lenin, who said that you can't make an omelette without breaking a few eggs — cultures have always commemorated some form of sacred violence in their origins, which they have considered a holy duty to renew....[18]

After the advent of the patriarchal, elitist society, the quiet greatness of archaic mystical experience turned into arrogant, loud, and intimidating grandiosity. If I am correct in suggesting this view, it seems consistent with the expectation that spiritual realization — whose nature transcends both the masculine and the feminine — might express itself differently in women and in men. Women's disposition had been mainly maternal, of course; and men's, biologically, had been more oriented towards aggressive domination and hunting. In a matristic context, therefore, spiritual experience would lead to an intensification of the communal bonds — the sense of the social, ecological, and even the cosmic "we" — whereas in a patriarchal context spiritual experience would justify an intensification of intellectual as well as domineering and aggressive tendencies.

And so even at the individual level, spiritual experience may lead a person to the discovery of a condition of profound equality with everything and everyone; or, alternatively, to feelings of spiritual superiority, producing a sense of entitlement compatible with exploitation, hegemony, and "holy war." I assume that the myths which speak about the deterioration of consciousness from the Silver Age to the heroic Bronze Age do not lie. Notwithstanding, the profound truth of this fall has been hidden behind the mask of superiority that serves the will to power and dominion.

Thus, Apollo might well have been the god of justice, the oracles, inspiration, harmony, purification, and self-awareness; but during his youth, we are told, he was also an aggressive conqueror like his father, the powerful, thundering Zeus. His arrows may well symbolize the light that triumphs over darkness and defeats monsters; but the justice, goodness, or virtue of shooting his arrows against the great serpent Python are not as obvious to us. (Had not Python been appointed by the Earth Mother to guard her oracle?) Apollo slays her with his arrows and takes over the oracle that would continue to be the center of Greek life.

And did Medusa, portrayed as a monster with serpents for hair, deserve to die? She and her sisters point us to the world of the Great Goddess, the spirit of nature; and it would seem that — with the arrival of the Olympian gods — the Great Mother was criminalized, just as Troy was criminalized for its complicity in kidnapping beautiful Helen, the wife of King Agamemnon, by Paris, the son of the noble Priam. I deliberately echo Homer in calling him "noble," for Homer sang of the nobility of the Trojans and their "sacred citadel" at the same time that he sang of Achilles' all-too-"heroic" determination to win. The nearly invincible Achilles is so greatly admired that usually he is assumed to be Homer's favorite hero. However, the *Iliad* is more a tragedy than a comedy, the deeds recounted in it being more sorrowful than joyous. Indeed, the *Iliad* teaches us much more about the immaturity of the heroic ideal than about the journey of purification taken by the hero to reach maturity (which is the theme of the *Odyssey*). There is nothing noble about Homer's portrayal of Achilles, the invincible and narcissistic superhero of that ruthless conquest. Nobler, clearly, is the portrait that Homer gives us of Hector, Priam's son, whom Achilles slays — and of the Trojans in general.

The Greeks considered the Trojan War to be the end of the Heroic Age and the beginning of the Iron Age. Everything suggests that matriarchal values persisted in Trojan culture, and that Troy was one of approximately three hundred cities that fell to the Indo-European invasions of the period. It is in keeping with this view that the beautiful queen of the Amazons, Penthesilea, fought with the Trojans. If we wish to understand Achilles' psychological makeup, then we must follow him empathetically when, battling the Amazon Penthesileia, he falls in love with her, cuts off her head, and rapes her corpse. This is all part of the heroic ideal, as is the ecstasy of the warrior and the search for glory. Yes: pleasure from violence and its conquests that confirms one's own grandiosity.

The Greeks invented the word *hubris* (usually translated as "arrogance or lack of measure") to mean precisely the arrogance and excess that I have been discussing. They were so interested in this complication of the encounter of the human mind with the divine world that the phenomenon came to constitute a *theme de rigueur* in their tragedies. Indeed, how could it possibly be otherwise? Every tragedy, like the myth of Dionysus (to whom all tragedies are dedicated), echoes the great journey of the soul.

Thus we find, in the first tragedy that Sophocles dedicates to Oedipus, the typical signs of this grandiosity that typically precedes a downfall. From the very beginning, the king in *Oedipus Rex* is portrayed as the greatest of all mortals, the man who has solved the riddle of the Sphinx and brought well-being to his people. After a deadly plague is unleashed on the land, Oedipus is determined to purify his city — as Apollo, through his oracle, indicates he should — and commands that the culprit be sought and punished. Yet in the end, he will discover that the culprit is no other than himself. And at this point, with the end of the play, we may say that his hubris has been punished, and he enters the legendary "valley of the shadow of death."

Oedipus Rex reads like a detective novel in which the detective discovers the unthinkable truth that he himself is the murderer. But it is also the story of a process of self-awareness that, for Freud, understandably mirrored the process of self-discovery in psychoanalysis.

Self-knowledge, then, leads Oedipus from self-exaltation to self-deprecation, and from *hubris* to a "dark night of the soul" that will end for him only twenty years later, with his apotheosis in the sacred grove of the Eumenides in Colonus.

To assert, as I do here, that *civilization itself is hubris* implies that we find in its unfolding something like a spiritual adolescence, a collective equivalent of the over-excited consciousness when "spirit goes to a person's head." In the same way that it can be accepted as normal that signs of immaturity in an arrogant adolescent bring complications, we might likewise take it to be normal and unavoidable that a pathology be involved in the spiritual immaturity of a society. How tragic, however, is the *collective* expression of hubris! As we understand how we came to feel ourselves to be the "masters of creation" through an adolescent excess in our ancient history, let us hope we also can understand that until we collectively comprehend the immaturity of this idea, our attachment to our immaturity will continue to cost us dearly.

The fundamental myth of our western Christian civilization is the Book of Genesis, which shows us man in his full stature as lord and master of nature, created in the own image of the almighty Lord of the universe. Here, patriarchal culture is defined precisely by its mastery over nature, which is symbolized in Genesis not only by the garden but also by the serpent winding through its pastures, by the apple, and by the woman. She is implicitly regarded as more predisposed than man to the natural order, and thus is placed in the role of the temptress.

Universal mythology tells us how the hero places a triumphant foot on top of the dragon's head, symbolizing through this gesture the liberation from evil and the triumph of spirit over our passionate and egocentric little ego. But when God announces that Eve will crush the serpent's head with her heel, we feel that the struggle of good against evil is invoked as a rationalization for the fundamental (and secretly criminal) gesture of patriarchy, which is the crushing of instinct — a turning against life itself through its vilification.

It is tempting to say that only the sublime *content* of the Books of Moses matters, and therefore we shouldn't pay too much attention to the patriarchal character of its style and symbolic language. But I fear that the patriarchal authoritarianism of the Mosaic theocracy, along with its ideology of "the chosen people" — far from being a mere detail — has constituted the direct source of the inquisitorial authoritarianism of the Christian church, and the indirect source of Muslim fanaticism. Nor has sectarianism been limited to western religions. For their compulsion to conquer in the name of a self-proclaimed superior spirituality has inspired the atrocious nationalisms of the modern world, along with their corresponding secular ideologies that demand hegemony in the name of high-resounding ideals and the "noble" cause of ridding the world of evildoers.

We may speak about deception, rationalization, or confusion in the civilizing rhetoric of the Greeks as well as in the Pentateuch, depending upon the degree to which we consider the concealment of a violent meaning behind a glorious one to be a conscious act. Yet whatever the case may be, what *is* true is that confusion is perpetuated through unconsciousness, which is why it is in our best interest to bring such masked violence out into the open. The deception is further complicated by its reference to the concept of the State, which defines itself as much by the "sum total of its citizens" as by "those who govern." In this way, when "the interests of the State" are invoked for this or that policy, we are led to believe that this refers to the democratic will of the people.

Until now, I have discussed the origins of our barbarian civilization and the concept of *hubris*. And I believe that these ideas entail a greater healing potential than those that speak simply of a "solar stage" in the development of consciousness, as Neumann and Wilber do. For rather than remaining fixed upon the arrogant adolescent will to omnipotence, it would be in our best interest to de-idealize ourselves and to permit expression of the social criticism that we have been repressing, in a cultural war against our Marxist heritage and the spirit of youth.

But perhaps speaking of *hubris* does not take us far enough into the past to truly understand the nature of our original grandiose exaltation. Explaining it as a complication of mystical development is the same as saying that among the ancients, just as in all times and all cultures (including the Zoroastrian drinkers of *Haoma*, who apparently institutionalized the holy war), proximity with the world of the divine has caused the more dissatisfied ones and those most driven by a thirst for glory to indulge in that misappropriation of spiritual energy that Jesus warned his disciples about when he said that it is best not to allow the left hand to know what the right hand is doing.

But what was the original dissatisfaction that led to such intense oppression of women and children?

Just as the spiritual novice undergoes an early illuminative stage, indulging such arrogant excesses to the extent that his grandiosity compensates an earlier frustration, so we may imagine that when the early Indo-Europeans waged war upon those whom they regarded as inferior barbarians and thus stepped up their collective neurosis into a collective and delusional mystical psychosis, they were projecting their angry frustration onto divine justice. When we look with Freudian eyes at the myth of Oedipus, we see how the cruel abandonment of the newborn leads to unconscious acts of parricide and incest. To put this in more universal terms: when the time of incipient spiritualization comes and we feel empowered by a glimpse of the divine, our early suffering seems to appeal to divine vengeance.

In addition to what I have explained concerning the need to suppress tenderness and women in order to survive through war in an increasingly impoverished land, and the cultural transmission of an inhibition of desire that originally resulted from chronic hunger, I think that Leonard Shlain's[19] reconstruction of the prehistory of the relationship between the sexes gives us additional insight. Shlain proposes that it was women who first understood the relationship between sex and pregnancy, as well as the considerable dangers of child-bearing; and he imagines that they also must have understood the importance of looking for security and protection in the future fathers of their children.

It is not too difficult to accept that women domesticated not only plants and animals but also, in their tender way, the males of the species. And it was mainly because of their influence, I imagine, that we have made the cultural evolution from the typical dominant male behavior of the anthropoids to a personality that has integrated something of the maternal spirit of women, and thus come to relate towards his children, partners, and closest kin in some kind of empathic and protective way.

But it is also easy to imagine that after a few millennia of adaptation to a matriarchal tribal spirit (at least in the Fertile Crescent), the masculine spirit began to feel paralyzed in the face of the Great Mother, with her control of the tribe and her tribal interpretation of the natural order. Rebelling, then, against this paralyzing tribal spirit, men must have felt driven by something like the intuition of a cosmic will of masculine liberation — even at the cost of the most horrible violence — against the breast that nourished them.

When Erich Fromm spoke of the matriarchy as a time of "incestuous union with the earth,"[20] he surely intuited that the coming of the patriarchal world was an evolutionary necessity. In this, I think he is closer to the truth than those who idealize the Neolithic as Earthly Paradise.

Our Cro-Magnon ancestors lived in the precarious Ice Age. Undoubtedly, the fierce threat to their survival contributed to the hardening of their hearts not only at that time, but also continued to do so even after they had settled into sedentary life. Yet if the filiarchal hunter-gatherers, in spite of their cult of the Great Mother, had already developed an excessive greed that entailed the distortion of healthy instinct and foreshadowed modern individualism, we may also conjecture that the first sedentary peoples probably outdid themselves in their efforts to survive through a collectivist excess. It is easy to understand the exaltation of individual initiative and masculine strategy as a valid liberation from such matristic tyranny, and this is coherent with the myth of Perseus conquering Medusa, and of Apollo defeating Python.

We may thus understand that the masculine community of the archaic patriarchy had emotional antecedents for feeling the necessity to defend their freedom of expression, even if it meant going against women and nature. And it is also conceivable that by perceiving women as their enemy, men hardened themselves to their own emotions and desires, attempting to turn ascetic — in terms not only of their own carnal desires, but also of their need for tenderness — in their pursuit of autonomy. It is believed that during the period of the first Neolithic villages, a portion of the population chose a rebellious and nomadic lifestyle. If this was so, then the matriarchal culture and the patriarchal option would have risen simultaneously out of the more anarchic social order of the primitive hunter-gatherers.

A few years ago, Dr. Warren Farrell, in his book *The Myth of Male Power*, proposed that feminism is wrong to protest male power, because it is the male sex, in fact, that is most victimized. After observing that the word "hero" means "servant," he brought forth abundant statistics to document the suffering caused to men by the sacrifice of seeing to war and other inconveniences. Yet it seems ludicrous to pretend, through such intellectual sleight of hand, to gloss over the millennia of masculine oppression of women, children, and men themselves throughout history. What *is* of interest in his presentation, rather, is that the facts confirm that men *also* suffer in patriarchal society.

It is true that the life expectancy of men is shorter than that of women. It is also true that men's lives are more alienated than women's, because of their dedication to money and the state. And it would seem that the takeover of power through which men hoped to protect themselves from women, as well as take their revenge on them, constituted only one level of their mental life, which was superimposed on an unconscious but effective archaic pattern of chivalrous and no less compulsive protectiveness. Yet it is also true that men suffer not only from a shorter time span and war mutilations, but mainly from loss of meaning, arrested psychological growth, poverty, injustice, and the other ills of patriarchal society that affect us all.

But now I shall take leave of these reflections, through which I sought to put together what we now know, with Tótila Albert's claim: that filiarchy, matriarchy, and patriarchy have been necessary for the development of our species, however destructively obsolete we find them today.

CHAPTER 4

PATRIARCHY TODAY

Rats and roaches live by competition under the law of supply and demand; it is the privilege of human beings to live under the laws of justice and mercy.

— Wendell Berry

The Nobodies
The nobodies: nobody's children, owners of
　nothing.
The nobodies: the no ones, made into nobodies,
Running like rabbits, dying through life, screwed
　every which way
Who are not, but could be.
Who don't speak languages, but dialects.
Who don't have religions, but superstitions.
Who don't create art, but handicrafts.
Who don't have culture, but folklore.
Who are not human beings, but human resources.
Who do not have faces, but arms.

Who do not have names, but numbers.
Who do not appear in the history of the world
   but in the police blotter of the local paper.
The nobodies, who are not worth the bullet that
   kills them.

— Eduardo Galeano

ALL EVIDENCE TELLS US THAT our collective life began as a filiarchy under the *aegis* of eros — instinctive wisdom — and the joy of freedom: an animal filiarchy, truly, that lasted during the earliest times of humankind; but we may imagine that in view of the need to survive the hunger and harshness of the last ice age, an originally harmonious anarchy eventually turned into an exploitive and crypto-cannibalistic individualistic excess.

Then it seems that there came a time when the brutality of the voraciously degraded Inner Child of our species underwent a process of socialization and refinement during the dawn of the early Neolithic matristic age (at least in the case of our Aryan and Semitic ancestors, who were tribal before turning despotic) — until, with the increasing drought, we may imagine that the more autarchic men, who had apparently resisted sedentary life from the beginning, sparked off the collective aggression towards agricultural societies (symbolized by the tale of Cain and Abel) that finally led to patriarchy.

Tribal chieftains, it seems, were originally guided by shamans. And the first kings were guided by priests, up to the moment of the independence of the despotic Priestly Kings. Their era was followed by that of the Empires, with their respective official churches.

I need not go into detail about the familiar history of the times between the French Revolution and the Napoleonic

Empire — when the bourgeoisie superseded the power of the old nobility, and republics began to emerge, along with their democratic ideals. It is enough to understand that this shift of power foreshadowed our own epoch, in which society is no longer under the rule of churches or of governments, but rather the supreme power lies in money and the international organization of business.

The "roaring twenties" ushered in the "Business Age," and since then the power of money has continued to increase. With the rise of the global economy in the 1980s, this Business Age has reached its full stature, and it is now an implicit trans-national empire, dominated by the market spirit to such an extent that all traditional values have been thrown into question, virtue has become an unrealistic aspiration of the past, and many would readily sell their grandmother in exchange for a suitable amount of electronic money.

How ridiculous the development of history would seem to us if it were to come to an end in our time!

Having shifted from an anarchic-instinctive and filiocentric Palaeolithic Age to the matristic Silver Age of the early Neolithic, then to the Heroic Age of the celestial divinities, and eventually onward to the degenerated patriarchy of the Iron Age — and having gone, in the course of this Iron Age or *Kali Yuga*, from an era of religious authority to one of military dominion, and on to a hybrid of meritocracy and scientific control dictated by experts — we have now come to an *age of business and propaganda*. In this age, all values, including that of life, wane before the value of money; and supreme author-

ity has come to rest, supposedly, on "the market" — shorthand
for the wants of an information-manipulated community and
the interests of giant trans-national companies united by the
agreements of global economy. This certainly doesn't appear
to be the fulfillment of our human potential!

Our day and age has been said to be one of Occidental-
ism (referring to the ferocious, financial triumph of Western
modernity over alternative cultures or societies). Yet it boils
down to nothing more than the old, reactivated patriarchal
spirit — which does not stop short of genocide, the destruction of entire cultures, or the invisible but chronic holocaust
brought about by its economic decisions.

In our times of violence, hyper-conformity, corruption,
and superficiality, it is no longer *the unfaithful* who are at-
tacked, for the secular society has grown tired of the faithful.
Rather, it is those who are not willing to echo the patriotism
über alles sentiment who bear the brunt of societal criticism.
Yet there is little difference between those who used to raise
flags in the name of God and those who cause bombs to fall in
the name of democracy. For, ironically, the higher values lend
themselves very well to promoting questionable policies. In the
meantime, the patriarchal system continues to perfect itself
— in part through technological development — so that now
a faceless, systemic despotism has brought us under its power
more than ever, and has managed to make us feel "free," even
as we toil for sustenance in an ever-more-enslaving market.

But we should not allow our intellectual and technological
progress to fool us by thinking that our minds have signifi-

cantly evolved since the times of our cannibalistic ancestors in the last Ice Age. For the cannibalistic attitude adopted at that remote time has since carried over into our exploitive and intrinsically anti-spiritual economy — evident in the increasing subordination of political power to money, and of the common people to the will of the rich. And as for its destructiveness, it has not lessened but instead has become incomparably greater.

In his book, *The Rise of the Network Society*, Manuel Castells[1] proposes that the vast and continuous transactions in the tidal wave of virtual money are most characteristic of the last phase of capitalism. As I purport to characterize "patriarchy today," however, I want to point out three aspects of the most recent metamorphosis of patriarchal power. The first could be called "institutional impunity," or systemic corruption. The second, I will call "the crypto-fascist character of the contemporary world." Lastly, since no reflection may be made about the characteristics of today's world without taking into account the prominent place that the USA occupies within it, I need to include this matter, too, in the present discussion.

In regard to systemic corruption, I quote the Uruguayan writer Eduardo Galeano, who has called our times an "upside-down world." Galeano claims that this upside-down world is "a school that rewards in reverse":

> It scorns honesty, punishes work, prizes lack of scruples, and feeds cannibalism. Its professors slander nature: injustice, they say, is the law of nature. Milton Friedman, one of the most prestigious members of the teaching body, speaks of the "natu-

ral rate of unemployment." By law of nature, Richard Herrn-
stein and Charles Murray verify, blacks are listed on the lowest
rung of the social ladder. To explain his business success, John
D. Rockefeller used to say that nature rewards the fittest and
punishes the useless. And more than a century later, many
owners of the world continue to believe Charles Darwin wrote
his book to announce their glory.

Galeano points out that when we speak of "survival of the
fittest," we are talking about the *killing instinct*. This is considered a virtue when "used by the big companies to digest small
companies and for strong countries to devour weak ones," but
"if any poor guy out of a job goes out in search of food with
a knife in his hand, it is the evidence of brutality." Thus, "the
good-for-nothing crook learns what he knows by raising his
eyes from the bottom to the heights; he studies the example of
the winners." He concludes that "a banker who sucks dry all
the money of a bank has the same chance of peacefully enjoying the benefits of his effort as a thief has of robbing a bank
and ending up in prison or the cemetery."

Galeano draws attention to how language is used to promote this double standard. "When a criminal kills someone
for an unpaid debt," he writes, "the execution is called a *settling
of accounts*; when the international technocracy settles accounts
with an indebted country, the execution is called an *adjust-
ment plan*." More universally, however, he indicts the world
economy as "the most efficient expression of organized crime,"
and claims that "the international bodies that control currency,
trade, and credit practice terrorism against poor countries, and
against the poor of all countries, with a cold-blooded profes-
sionalism and impunity that would make the best of bomb
throwers turn red."

This implies that swindling has become acceptable, "when some successful politicians stretch their talent. In the suburbs of the world, the chiefs of state sell the leftover scraps of their countries at end-of-season sale prices, much as criminals in the city suburbs sell, at despicable prices, the spoils of their raids. The hit men who are hired to kill on a minor scale, perform the same duties that are performed on a large scale by generals decorated for crimes that are elevated to the category of military triumphs."

I conclude my reference to Galeano's indictment with the following summary:

> In such an upside-down world, the countries that guard the peace also make and sell the most weapons to other countries; the most prestigious banks launder the most amount of drug money and harbor the most stolen cash; the most successful industries are the most poisonous to the planet; and saving the environment is the brilliant business endeavor of the companies that profit from annihilating it. Those who kill the most people in less time, make the most money with less work, and who exterminate the greatest amount of nature at the lowest cost are worthy of impunity and a pat on the back.[2]

Fascism is also an expression of patriarchy that seems to be perfecting itself and gaining ground in the contemporary world. Shortly after Nixon was elected, I recall how Fritz Perls, who had long resided at Esalen, in Big Sur, California, decided to move to Canada. He explained that since he had already come to know fascism in Germany only too well, he was quick to recognize the symptoms, and felt the time to change residence had come for him once again.

What did Perls mean by "fascism"? It was more than the mere loss of liberty in a conventional and repressive world. I imagine that he referred to a certain mentality, whose nature psychologists had taken on the task of clarifying since the 1940s.

The investigations began in the aftermath of Nazi Germany, with a group called "the Frankfurt School." This was a group of remarkable people who had been deeply influenced by both Marx and Freud. It included Theodor Adorno, Max Horkheimer, Herbert Marcuse, Erich Fromm, and Wilhelm Reich.

Reich emphasized mostly the repressive aspect of fascism. He pointed out that the unnaturalness of subjection to non-humanitarian authority tended to involve not only a loss of openness to pleasure and sensory experience, but also a loss of inwardness. It is this loss of inwardness that explains the loss of creativity in fascistic regimes, as well as their antagonism to higher culture.

Later on in America, the ideas of the Frankfurt School inspired an ambitious research project on ethnocentrism, which came to focus on the personality of those who are inclined to a fascist ideology. This, in turn, resulted in the publication of a thick book, *The Authoritarian Personality*,[3] which had a widespread influence in the academic community, as evidenced by the research reported in American psychological journals during the following two decades or so. The research described throughout the pages of *The Authoritarian Personality* included interviews, testing, and psychodynamic interpretation. One of its outcomes was a questionnaire called the *F scale*, a psychometric instrument intended to identify individuals with a fascism-prone personality.

General features of such "Authoritarian Personality" (as it was called) included the following traits:

- "authoritarian aggression" (directed to subordinates and outgroups);
- "authoritarian submission" (submission before established authorities);
- a severe or punitive (and repression-inducing) super-ego;
- superstition; and
- an "alienated *id*" (an expression indicating a manner of experiencing or interpreting impulses, in which the individual feels that his "weaknesses" are not himself or of his own doing — as in saying, "I don't know what overtook me").

In one of the book's chapters, Adorno described various distinct syndromes present among the high scorers of the F scale. And later research involving the sophisticated statistical method known as *factor analysis* has demonstrated that the "authoritarian-personality" population actually is comprised of three different personality types. Yet this does not detract from the psychodynamic findings, or from the understanding of fascist ideology as a result of both political will and predisposing personality factors.

Since the days of the Frankfurt School, the world has given rise to yet more fascist regimes. Furthermore, we may observe a transformation of fascism, as it becomes perfected through technology and the use of the media. In a recent article, Lawrence Britt[4] has formulated the common characteristics of fascism in light of a study of seven different systems: Hitler's Germany; Mussolini's Italy; Franco's Spain; Salazar's Portugal; Suharto's Indonesia; Papadopoulos' Greece; and Pinochet's

Chile. He found "striking similarities in modus operandi" among them all.

Looking at the traits common to national behavior and abuse of power in the cited regimes provides us with a more detailed vision of the phenomenon on a collective level. Here is a list of these traits, adapted from Britt's article:

1. *Powerful and continuing expressions of nationalism.* Prominent displays of flags, pride in the military, and demands for unity were common themes in the expression of this nationalism, which was usually coupled with a suspicion of things foreign that often bordered on xenophobia.

2. *Disdain for the importance of human rights.* "The regimes themselves viewed human rights as of little value and a hindrance to realizing the objectives of the ruling elite," Britt writes. "Through clever use of propaganda, the population was brought to accept these human rights abuses by marginalizing, even demonizing, those being targeted."

3. *Identification of enemies/scapegoats as a unifying cause.* The most significant common thread among these regimes was the use of scapegoating as a means to divert people's attention from other problems, to shift blame for failures, and to channel frustration in controlled directions. Active opponents of these regimes were inevitably labeled as "terrorists," and dealt with accordingly.

4. *Supremacy of the military/avid militarism.* Ruling elites always identified closely with the military and the industrial infrastructure that supported it. A dispropor-

tionate share of national resources was allocated to the military, even when domestic needs were acute. The military was seen as an expression of nationalism, and was used whenever possible to assert national goals, intimidate other nations, and increase the power and prestige of the ruling elite.

5. *Rampant sexism.* Beyond the simple fact that the political elite and the national culture were male-dominated, these regimes inevitably viewed women as second-class citizens. They were adamantly anti-abortion and also homophobic. These attitudes were usually codified in Draconian laws that enjoyed strong support by the orthodox religion of the country, thus lending the regime a cover for its abuses.

6. *Control of the mass media.* "Under some of the regimes, the mass media were under strict direct control and could be relied upon never to stray from the party line." Methods included the control of licensing and access to resources, economic pressure, appeals to patriotism, and implied threats.

7. *Obsession with national security.* "Inevitably, a national security apparatus was under direct control of the ruling elite. It was usually an instrument of oppression, operating in secret and beyond any constraints." Also, "questioning its activities was portrayed as unpatriotic or even treasonous."

8. *Linking religion and the ruling elite.* The fact that the ruling elite's behavior was incompatible with the precepts of the religion was generally swept under the rug. Propaganda kept up the illusion that the ruling

elites were defenders of the faith and opponents of the "godless." "A perception was manufactured that opposing the power elite was tantamount to an attack on religion."

9. *Protection of the power of corporations.* Although the personal life of ordinary citizens was under strict control, the ability of large corporations to operate in relative freedom was not compromised. The ruling elite saw the corporate structure as not only a way to ensure military production (in developed states), but also as an additional means of social control.

10. *Suppression or elimination of the power of labor.* "Since organized labor was seen as the one power center that could challenge the political hegemony of the ruling elite and its corporate allies, it was inevitably crushed or made powerless." "The poor formed an underclass, viewed with suspicion or outright contempt. Under some regimes, being poor was considered akin to a vice."

11. *Disdain and suppression of intellectuals and the arts.* "Intellectuals and the inherent freedom of ideas and expression associated with them were anathema to these regimes." "Intellectual and academic freedom were considered subversive to national security and the patriotic ideal."

12. *Obsession with crime and punishment.* "Most of these regimes maintained Draconian systems of criminal justice, with huge prison populations. The police were often glorified and had almost unchecked power, leading to rampant abuse.... Fear, and hatred, of criminals

or 'traitors' was often promoted among the population as an excuse for more police power."

13. *Rampant cronyism and corruption.* "Those in business circles and close to the power elite often used their position to enrich themselves. This corruption worked both ways; the power elite would receive financial gifts and property from the economic elite, who in turn would gain the benefit of government favoritism. Members of the power elite were in a position to obtain vast wealth from other sources as well: for example, by stealing national resources."

14. *Fraudulent elections.* "Elections in the form of plebiscites or public opinion polls were usually bogus. When actual elections with candidates were held, they would usually be perverted by the power elite to get the desired result."

As early as the beginning of the twentieth century, John Dewey pointed out the essence of the developing fascist phenomenon when he observed that "politics is the shadow cast on society by big business." Yet however much the fascist mentality or "authoritarian personality" may be a factor in promoting fascist regimes — and however much these, in turn, may stimulate the development of the individual fascist mind — fascism, it would seem, needs to be understood in the context of history as a whole. It represents merely a late development of an alliance between power and technology that was the hallmark of the Iron Age from its beginnings. In recent times, the influence of industrialists is no longer mediated by lobbying. They have come to sit in parliaments, and the whole world has come under the rule of the abstract programs of the trans-national corporations that arose from the activity of the more successful entrepreneurs — programs that are variations on the general principle of putting profits before people.

But now let me turn to a consideration of the third characteristic of modernity that I have posed: the central position of the USA in the world.

According to Gunnar Adler-Karlsson (the Swedish creator of the Capri Philosophical Park, in his guide to this park[5]), our social world may be seen as a solar system in formation, in which the United States of North America is the sun around which all other nations revolve like planets. And it is certainly true that, following the Cold War, the USA has attained an unprecedented hegemonic power. Furthermore, in the name of an alleged socio-cultural superiority, it has appointed itself as an international police force, committed to the military protection of a world supposedly threatened by anti-democratic interests. Adler-Karlsson's opinion is that, since genetically we are predators and "history is a violent game of elimination that tends to diminish the A/P ratio (between the affluent and the poor)," it is a good thing that we do have a super-police force.

Yet there clearly are others who regret that a culture in decline has been elevated to the supreme power in the world, and who believe that the highly praised rhetoric of the "defense of democracy" is nothing more than a paternalistic recourse of imperialism, similar to that which has been used so many times throughout history. These critics question the moral or cultural superiority that the United States attributes to itself in its pretense of justifying its power. Some have even claimed that the notion of the USA as a "guardian of democracy" is a myth cultivated by the news media.

Michael Ventura,[6] for example, has drawn attention to the statistics on mathematical literacy, so valued by North American educational policy. Surprisingly, in a comparative study among forty countries, the U.S. ranks a low 28th. According to exam scores of people with fewer than nine years of education, Americans were among the worst. Furthermore, this rich country ranks 54th in terms of fairness of health care, according to the World Health Organization. Lack of medical insurance coverage is the cause of 18,000 American deaths every year, and American women have a 70 percent higher risk of dying in childbirth than do women in Europe. The principal cause of death among pregnant American women is murder. On the other hand, according to *Global Finance*, "all the leading companies except for one are European." Thus, Ventura concludes that the USA is "number one" only in military power, consumerism, environmental destruction, and external debt.

In their book *The Good Society*,[7] Robert Bellah, et al. remark: "Some people insist that it is unpatriotic to say that America is no longer Number One; the whole idea smacks of defeatism and breeds a lack of confidence unworthy of a great nation... but few people ask, What does it mean to be Number One in an interdependent world?"

Toward the end of a chapter entitled "America in the World," they write:

> The United States of America is still the strongest and wealthiest nation in this world. With its economic and political strength come great responsibilities to build the foundation for order, stability and rising prosperity. But its power is no longer

sufficient for it easily to impose its will to its allies, much less to its rivals. To maintain peace it will have to cooperate more readily with other nations than it is used to doing....

It would be a mistake, for instance, to abandon all caution with regard to agreements for nuclear and conventional arms control. But it would be a tragedy not to take advantage of opportunities for arms control simply because our economy is addicted to a huge defense industry. And it would be self-destructively foolish to fail to deal with remediable causes of the brutal poverty afflicting so much of the world. To a significant degree, this poverty is the result of an economic system that favors the wealthiest countries at the expense of the poorest.... It is in no way a matter of starry-eyed idealism to advocate an alleviation of poverty through reform of the institutions governing international finance....

Noam Chomsky begins his book, *Failed States: The Abuse of Power and the Assault on Democracy*, with the observation that nothing threatens our collective survival more than nuclear war, environmental disaster, and "the fact that the government of the world's leading power is acting in ways that increase the likelihood of these catastrophes." He also sees a deep division between public opinion and the policies of the nation in question — to such an extent that there is reason to fear that "the American system as a whole is heading in a direction that spells the end of its historical values of equality, liberty and *meaningful democracy*."[8]

Several critics of the betrayal of American ideals by those who rhetorically claim to enforce them have written books in whose title one finds the expression "the Beast," the apocalyptic symbolism of which would make America into a new Babylon. However, as appropriate as this old designation may be in reference to patriarchy's power and destructiveness, I think it would be a mistake to think of *any* government today as more than a puppet of trans-national business interests. Also, true as it may be that an alliance has been established between American imperialism and the designs of a faceless Empire, I don't think we should consider the U.S. to be more than the Empire's powerful right arm. If we are looking for the true face of the Beast, it is time to look beyond nations. As Cicero made clear, nations come and go, but power remains the same. A complex of exploitation, obscurantism, and deception has controlled the whole world for ages; and now it does this so thoroughly that for the first time it seems to have reached its full stature, so that we may clearly discern its monstrous features.

CHAPTER 5

THE PATRIARCHAL MIND

Throughout history, the really fundamental changes in societies have come about not through the
dictates of governments and the results of battles
but through vast numbers of people changing their
minds — sometimes only a little bit.

— Willis Harman, *Global Mind Change*

IF WE TAKE SERIOUSLY THE NOTION that a *deterioration* of our
consciousness constitutes the crux of our crisis-ridden patriarchal society, then we should understand that nothing could
be of greater service to the evolution of society than a massive *improvement* of people's consciousness. Yet change requires
deep understanding; and thus, in this chapter, I will undertake
to reflect further about the problematic patriarchal consciousness that we so urgently need to overcome.

If we consider this degradation of our consciousness to be no more than a simple "exaltation of the ego," we are not saying enough. Of course, the word *ego* is useful because of its multiple meanings: neurosis, insular consciousness, egoism, arrogance, voracity, loss of contact with a deeper identity, and so on. And yet a word in which so many meanings converge falls short of leading us to the silenced root of our multi-faceted *problematique*.

Thus, I prefer to be more specific about this ignored and dismissed root at the center of our problems, and to call it the *patriarchal mind*, or the *patristic ego* — expressions that seem a more accurate way to refer to the complex of violence, excess, grandiosity, and insensitivity that arose when our ancestors, faced with the survival crisis that supervened some six thousand years ago, were forced into becoming migrating predatory warriors.

I have said throughout this book that a "patriarchal mind" underlies the patriarchal problem of society. Yet I have barely begun to characterize this mind through words such as "violence" and "insensitivity," and the observation that relationships of dominance-submission and paternalism-dependency have interfered with the capacity to establish cooperative and brotherly and sisterly adult bonds. Or, to put it another way: the patriarchal mind is one in which the thirst for maternal and paternal love has led to an emotional dependency and a compulsive obedience that not only alienate but also constitute distortions, falsifications, and caricatures of love.

Just as the *paterfamilias* has dominated over "his" wife and "his" children in the *external* family, so the repressive patriarchal voice of society has dominated *within* us over the voice of our Mother aspect and its matristic values, as well as over our "Inner Child." Inevitably, our way of life, our institutions, and our laws have emerged as crystallizations from this patriarchal mind. And now that we are all faced with an obsolescence crisis, we find ourselves urgently needing to reconsider this root pathology of consciousness so that we can leave it behind.

The dominance of the Absolute Father has been expressed in society, in culture, and throughout history through more than male chauvinism, alone. It has also manifested as the tyranny of reason over emotions and instinctual pleasure, and as an overvaluation of knowledge at the expense of love and freedom. Thus the aggression of the male adreno-maniacs of the world has punished and inhibited not only tenderness but also spontaneity and naturalness, robbing us of both love and authenticity. This aggressiveness has belittled and isolated us, interfering with the potential for brotherhood and sisterhood, without which a healthy society cannot flourish.

Although our understanding of the psychological world has emerged, in large part, through our comprehending its dysfunctions (i.e., emotional problems and their afflictions), we can also understand psycho-spiritual imbalances through a clear vision of what constitutes a *healthy* mind and society. Therefore, I will sketch out some further reflections on wholeness before proceeding.

Though it was clear to Tótila Albert that the "Inner Father" entails the intellect, just as the "Mother" entails love and the "Child" action, he insisted that these inner persons are more than simply their three associated psychic functions. And I am sure that he would celebrate the current discovery that thinking, feeling, and doing correspond with three territories in our neuro-anatomy: the neocortex, the mid-brain, and the archaic brain.

What Gurdjieff had already prophetically described at the turn of the last century is well established today, thanks to the investigations of Paul MacLean, whose explorations have revealed the tri-partite structure of the human brain. As is currently well known, only the *neocortex* — which has a more recent evolutionary origin — can be considered the human brain proper; for we share our *relational* mid-brain with our mammalian ancestors, and our archaic *instinctual* brain resembles that of the reptiles.

In *The End of Patriarchy*, written in the 1980s, I described shamanism as the activity of exceptional individuals who — transcending the tyranny of their intellect, emotions, and habits — have reached the condition of truly three-brained beings. It is through the ability to love and the freedom of their inner "snake–power," I claimed at that time, that they are able to be healers.

Today, I would say that the tri-unification of the mind is the essence of self-realization. However, this crucial understanding of the process has been either neglected or else formulated in esoteric terms comprehensible only to those with rare teachings, such as that of the *Trikaya* of the *Vajrayana*, or the Mystery of the Trinity of Christian theology. Gurdjieff — that mysterious spiritual master whose work would come to have so much influence on my own work with groups — was the exception. At the turn of the last century, he created his "Institute for the Harmonious Development of Man" precisely in relation to the idea of the balance among the three centers of the personality.

Yet whereas Gurdjieff (as well as the pioneers of holistic education) took a special interest in the harmony among thinking, feeling, and doing, my personal interest has increasingly been that of the tri-une organization of human experience in reference to the three forms or aspects of love.

○

As I have proposed in my book, *Changing Education to Change the World*, father-love, or *philia*, is oriented towards the "heavenly" — i.e., towards the world of principles, ideas, and ideals. It is *father-love* that underlies the experience of value ascription, which characterizes respect, admiration, devotion, and — in its supreme degree — adoration.

Mother-love — whose characteristics are generosity and empathy, and whose supreme form is compassion — is, by contrast, oriented toward individual beings. It is stimulated not by merits, but by needs.

Child-love, the third aspect (exceedingly pathologized in our age, because the loving bond towards parents is complicated by an idealized dependency, by compulsive obedience, or by resentment) can be recognized in the elemental search for pleasure and, more broadly, in the free orientation towards happiness. We may call it "enjoyment-love," and identify child-love with *eros* — which, traditionally, is distinguished from both the maternal *agape* and from *philia*, the respectful or appreciative love that the father figure inspires in the child, and which is at the source of the drive to follow and learn.

Clearly, a balance among these three forms of love — which is equivalent to the notion of balance among our three brains — is an uncommon thing. Yet I am convinced that happiness and mental health depend on the fullness of this love-spectrum.

This was already implied in the Christian precept to love one's neighbor as oneself, and to love God above all things, which Jesus of Nazareth claimed summarized the essence of the Law of Moses. Yet we may say that the seeming oneness of that statement actually contains *three* injunctions: to love oneself, to love the other, and to love God. Furthermore, the love of oneself, the love of one's neighbor, and the love of God differ not only in their object but also in their experiential character. For it is implicitly understood that it is not *erotic* love that is being prescribed in the commandment to love one's neighbor. Similarly, we understand that it is *not* compassionate love that we should harbor towards God.

Love of one's neighbor constitutes an expression of *agape*, or kindness, while the love of the divine corresponds to the highest form of that appreciative love which Socrates and Aristotle called *philia*; and in the love of oneself — inevitably, a love of our "Inner Child" — we can recognize an interest in the happiness of our instinctual being, governed by its "pleasure principle" (that is to say, *eros*).

The Christian precept, then, amounts to an admonition to *balance* father-love with mother-love and child-love.

Yet the patriarchal condition may be described as one where the intellect, which orients itself towards ideal values, is culturally overvalued in comparison with the mother-domain of affection and the child-domain of instinct. Furthermore, this so-called intellectual love does not go beyond a somewhat rhetorical cult of, or lip-service to, such values. And so respectful love, now transformed into obligation, chokes the instinctual pleasure-love, and eclipses or becomes a substitute for true goodness or kindness. On an individual level, this is the case of so many "good people" in the civilized world, who are driven more by duty than by empathy or tenderness. And on a collective level, this distortion accounts for the great discord between our democratic rhetoric and our true capacity for justice and equity.

I think that in light of this new anthropology — suggested by modern neuro-anatomy — we can more accurately consider what I have thus far been calling the "patriarchal mind." In light of this model of health as the integration of our brains, inner persons, and aspects of love, let us further consider the fragmented mind that results from our common patriarchal up-bringing that constitutes the common condition of humanity.

Since this will lead us to a reinterpretation of current psychopathology from the viewpoint of a fragmentation among the "father," "mother," and "child" aspects of our psyche, it is fitting that I briefly spell out further my tri-partite vision of the mind. For although it does not completely coincide with the mind maps in current use, it is close enough to them to seem familiar to us.

At the dawn of scientific psychology, Franz Brentano had already formulated a tri-partite vision of the functions, or spheres, of the mind. Thus he drew our attention to how experience encompasses a cognitive aspect, an emotional aspect, and a third aspect — which he termed "conative" — comprising impulses, desires, will, and, ultimately, action.

I have already spoken of how these three aspects — like three inner voices sustaining the counterpoint of our psyche — are closely related to the three parts of our tri-unitary brain. But along with the two triads of our neuro-anatomical structure and of our three inner persons, we also need to consider the Freudian triad of "psychic instances." Freud conceived the neurotic mind as one in which a disagreement and antagonism reigns between the instinctive sphere (*id*) and the sphere of the internalized directives and expectations of society (*superego*), while the part of us that we experience as "I" (or *ego*) precariously tries to execute an integrating function in the midst of a chronic conflict between pleasure and reality, instinct and civilization. And since Freud, it has been through the lens of these concepts that most psychotherapists have examined psychic life.

The Freudian *superego* has been regarded not only as the seat of ideals, but also as a domain in which these ideals are fostered by the intellect's power of abstraction. And it can also be said that ideals and principles — as organizers of psychic life — entail a directive function that may be described as an implicit *authority*. All this suggests that our neocortex is not merely the seat of intellectual life, but also an entity more aptly described as a *sub-personality*: an inner voice in our mind, in which thinking may well be the main fact but by no means constitutes its entirety. This is why it may well be more satisfactory to speak of a "critical parent" (as Eric Berne later would) than simply of an "intellectual center." And given that it is mostly men (especially in the patriarchal world) who exercise authority, it is entirely appropriate that we call the superego the "Inner Father."

In much the same way, we can speak of the Freudian *id* as our Inner Child, since it represents the voice of unconditioned Nature within us. And we can speak of the Freudian *ego* as our Motherly aspect, inasmuch as it entails a loving mediation and constitutes the field for an integration between impulses and principles, between nature and society.

Therefore, we need no great change in perspective in order to move from the Freudian interpretation of neurosis as a conflict between the "psychic instances" (superego, id, and ego) to an understanding of emotional disturbances as the outcome of a dysfunctional inter-relationship between the "inner three," in response to the culturally transmitted patriarchal imperative of a tyranny of the neocortex (with its intellect turned into *superego*) over the instinctual realm and over the dictates of solidarity in the family or society.

No matter how people's character may differ in respect to the dominant function and the most underdeveloped function of the thinking-feeling-doing triad, we may say that overall, patriarchal culture entails a hegemony of the intellect. Patriarchy, since its beginnings, has been an ally of intellect and reason — simply because dictating what people should think or believe also controls what they do with their words and actions. If I control the *thoughts* of another, I also control *him*; for his thinking must be more or less coherent with what he feels and wants. Thus the humorous notion that "language must have been invented for the purpose of lying" holds quite true in the political world, where words and ideas are used not only to control others through indoctrination, but also to feign and conceal.

The authority of the first kings, without question, was accompanied by an *ideology* — reinforced, in turn, by awe-inspiring ceremonies — that affirmed the position of these monarchs as mediators of the divine/the cosmic order. And when this original spiritual authority was succeeded by secular authority, based on military power, that authority was also endorsed by ideology. This ideology has been regarded by sociologists as a "civil religion," forcing people into patriotically accepting the dogma of the goodness of the State and the nobility of civic duties.

Thus, there is no doubt that since the beginning of civilization, authority has been based on a particular vision of things. And, ironically, since the Age of Enlightenment — which we associate with great progress in freedom — the empire of reason has become so strong that science, empiricism, and expert authority have practically put an end to beauty, goodness, inspiration, and sacredness in our world.

Until recent times, science has occupied the place that was once held by religious authority. Yet increasingly, scientific knowledge has become *scientism*: the pretension that science can comprehend everything, and that whatever it does not comprehend simply does not exist. It may be argued that the idolatry of science underlies the modern idea that governing the world according to merely economic considerations and with the help of computation is, in itself, the wisest option. It also may be said to underlie the contemporary belief that considering the abstraction of *homo economicus* as being driven by self-interest makes it idle to address real human beings and the mysterious complexity of living humanity.

From another point of view, we can understand the patriarchal mind as an imbalance in the realm of love: an imbalance between *instinctual love*, directed toward pleasure; *caring or empathetic love* for one's neighbor; and *appreciative love*, whose ordinary expression is respect, and whose higher form is devotion. Although the formula or personal profile regarding the prominence of one or another of these three loves varies among different people, patriarchal culture leaves an imprint in all, and the result is a loss of integration.

The manner in which patriarchal civilization has turned against *eros* has been eloquently described by Eisler in her book, *Sacred Pleasure*. Here, she sees this antagonism symbolized in the vilification of the biblical serpent, and in the divine command to Eve (or was it simply a prophecy?) to crush the head of the serpent with her heel.*

The expulsion from Paradise in the Book of Genesis has been interpreted in various ways: as a step forward in an evolutionary journey; as an outcome of curiosity (e.g., by Kafka); as a punishment for the desire to be like God; or as a thirst for knowledge. But we cannot overlook associating Eden with the state of sexual innocence, for the first signal we are given that our ancestors fell into temptation is that Adam and Eve now *know* that they are naked, and attempt to cover themselves. It is not that the temptation has actually been sexual. It is that the fruit of the tree of "knowledge of good and evil" has entailed a judgment that makes *instinct* evil. And since eating of that fruit, not only did we become civilized, but it is also precisely the self-rejection of turning against instinct that causes us to consider ourselves to be so.

Aristophanes, in Plato's *Symposium*, attributed human dissatisfaction to our having been split into two, and that consequently we live seeking our other half. In truth, something like this has actually occurred — only not through a physical division, but through an invisible intra-psychic compartmentalization. Generation after generation, we are implicitly taught that nature must be domesticated, in the external world as much as in the internal world, and this implies the notion of an intrinsic evil, and a perception of nature as intrinsically foreign.

---

* "I will put enmities between thee and the woman, and thy seed and her seed: she shall crush thy head, and thou shalt lie in wait for her heel."

Today, we understand that in an epoch more ancient than that in which the biblical Genesis was recorded, the serpent symbolized the organismic wisdom of life — as absent from the patriarchal mind as it was sacred to our matristic ancestors. The various prehistoric images of a serpent alongside a tree, which have been taken to refer to a mythical paradise, convey to us the sense of immanent spirituality that our prehistoric forebears must have experienced before the advent of the religions of transcendence. And although these religions may have reflected a forward step in consciousness, they also created a context of masculine dominance that entailed a distancing from life and from experience.

It could be that the first transition from the religion of the great universal Mother to a religion centering around the masculine personification of the divine as a divine *ruler* took place in the moment when the mythic husband of the eternal goddess — dying and being reborn every year with the cycles of life — became the principal figure of that cult. It is very likely that this is how it happened with Adonis, Osiris, and Dionysus. However, in the following patriarchal era of the Olympian gods that succeeded the original Dionysian religion — and whose advent is commemorated by myths such as Apollo slaying the Python serpent (or Perseus decapitating the Gorgon Medusa) — it is understandable that Dionysus would take on the character of a marginal god, as in the myths that have reached us today.

The Great Goddess, nonetheless, persisted in the era of the Olympians, behind the masks of Aphrodite (born from the castration of Cronos), Hera (the jealous spouse of Zeus), and Athena (born from the head of the father of the gods). Yet it is noteworthy that the pantheon of the Immortals conceived by the Greeks did not include a *merciful* divinity, and that the

Greco-Roman gods, for the most part, had little or no interest in the welfare of humans. And even this culture, which represented its gods in the nude, began to turn its back on eros. What *is* exalted above all else, in this old patriarchal culture, is the love of the heroic ideal, with its implications of a conquering spirit, personal grandiosity, and patriotic duty — all expressions of the ruthless will of a warrior bent on triumph at the expense of life.

Moreover, although it is *natural* for a healthy child to love his loving parents, at some moment in history it was laid down that filial love had to be *compulsory*; and the sort of love that the law specified was none other than *respect* — as befits obedience to authority. For patriarchy *is* authority, through power and indoctrination; and the ancient governments were based upon paternalism. Part of patriarchy's authority came from what children granted to their progenitors — originally as a natural response to their parents' protection and, presumably, their superior knowledge. But already within the family, authoritarianism involved a distortion of emotional life through the exaltation of admiration and respect toward the father. More broadly, patriarchal society exalts the love of ideals (common to both the sense of duty and prohibitions) at the expense of empathic love, as well as the valuation of pleasure.

On an interpersonal level, authoritarianism represents a position that could be translated as: "You owe me respect, so you must recognize that I am right, because I am wiser than you." And, "Your actions must conform to my advice or will, even when this contradicts your own preferences or judgments." And, "You should not only lend me your ears and your mind, but hand over the whole of your behavior, allowing me to be the one who guides it." All this involves nothing less than seizing possession of the body of another.

A similar ethic exists on an emotional level: mere automatic obedience on the part of a child is not enough to satisfy an authoritarian father, who expects his child to be *pleased* to obey, and to obey out of "love." The child, then — feeling that he should *like* having to postpone his own preferences or opinions — is left with only one recourse: that of disassociating himself from his body (and from his true emotions) in the interest of what he *must* like and what he *should* feel. Therefore, in view of such emotional "possession," the prohibition of pleasure — or at least the devaluation of the instinctive and the erotic — is, understandably, intrinsic to the maintenance of authoritarianism.

And what happens to *compassion*, in the atmosphere of patriarchy?

To answer this question, we must affirm various things at the same time. Firstly, the history of civilization has been, roughly speaking, a history of brutality masked behind an idealization of heroism. If we imagine a fictitious Martian observing the events that have taken place on Earth through the centuries, it is easy to anticipate that he would conclude that humans, on the whole, are ruthless people, endowed with very little compassion.

No matter how decisive feminine empathy may have been in bringing about tribal society, our later history shows that male aggression has clearly militated against a more tender culture. (And the same can be said regarding the patriarchal imbalance between increasing competitiveness in the world and an ever-diminishing spirit of collaboration.) We may view our tendency to go to war as having emerged from hunting, but originally hunting was simply an act of survival and protection of family members. Just as hunting turned sadistic, so war has turned into a dangerous passion, and a powerful — and empowering — business.

Yet this is not all. Paradoxically, despite the aggressive environment of the patriarchal world, the subjugated feminine aspect within it has been highly prized — as is water in the desert, where it is scarce. Femininity is a very sweet thing in hard times; and precisely when its presence is in short supply, compassion becomes a cherished ideal.

Hoisting an *ideal* of compassion, however, is not the same as *being* compassionate. More accurately, our ideals contribute to our feeling that we are virtuous merely for adoring them, even though we fail to be faithful to them in our deeds. Did the act of praying to Mary — a symbolic incarnation of divine mercy — diminish the brutality of the Crusades? The Christian ideal of love, upheld as the banner of Christian civilization, has mostly contributed to disguise its increasingly hardened heart.

In the patriarchal system, love is prized not only as an ideal that we are, by definition, far from reaching, but also as something that serves our interests. For does not generosity allow itself to be exploited? When a conflict arises between two people, surely it is the more affectionate one who gives in, since whoever is more capable of empathy toward the needs of the other is more likely to relinquish his or her self-interest. Therefore, it is not surprising that an exploitive culture welcomes kindness, even when it is scarcely given to feeling it or fostering it.

Going deeper into our analysis of love in the patriarchal condition, we may say that our unrealized potential turns against us, and neurotic needs emerge from the void left by our insufficiency of loving. These needs may superficially pass for forms of love, but they are actually love-*derivatives*, which we very often confuse with love and which interfere with its true expression.

What we worship, in our patriarchal reality, is frequently not of this world, for it rises far beyond the typical insignificance of the ordinary human world. We can characterize it as "archetypal" or ideal — a reality apart, which we may perhaps associate with the realm of the divine. (So much does this happen that when we find the ideal incarnated in certain people, we can say that not only do we idolize them, but we actually divinize them.) Heroes — perhaps like the parents of our childhood, certain friends, and good statesmen — become authorities, whom we can perceive as quasi-divine mediators of a higher authority, or at least a spiritual influence.

Nietzsche perhaps exaggerated in saying that we are so concerned with heaven because we despise the earth, and that our enthusiasm for the ideal is a compensation for our incapacity of loving the real. Yet I think he was probably correct in observing that the rejection of the instinctive fosters our thirst for illusions. I do not doubt that the capacity to revere the living and the dead, to venerate life itself, and to appreciate all things between heaven and earth is the *most* human among human capacities. I even think that the most complete love is that in which lovers can intuitively sense the divine in the other (such that not only do they desire each other and wish for each other's well being but they also *adore* each other). Yet an excess of adoration often compensates for an inhibition of desire or a lack of charity. Something like a redirection of psychic energy can occur, such that the emptiness left by the inhibition of one or another of our loving abilities prompts the search for an alternative (though impossible) satisfaction. Thus, the contempt for pleasure and even for life itself — characteristic of warriors who are fully committed to banding together in an act perceived to be their patriotic duty — may be compensated by the furious and frenetic ecstasy that has so characteristically accompanied the gratification of the heroic ideal.

If we think of the form of love that drove Achilles and the other Homeric heroes who exalted the glory of death in battle so unfalteringly, we can say without a doubt that this has to do with the admiring love of ideals and the voice of authority. Yet this is less indicative of the loving capacity expressed in recognizing the value in the others (as is the case in devotion), than of a thirst for recognition and the corresponding zeal of sacrificing everything for fame. It is not difficult to see that for all his glitter, Achilles was a monster of narcissism: that is to say, one who — despite the prestige of being an incomparable hero — was led by the thirst for personal competitive triumph to acts of supreme inhumanity.

Although the excellence of admiring love is so well celebrated by poets like Homer, who knew how to sing the virtues of heroes and venerate those who deserved praise for their wisdom, goodness, or justice, we would not say that an Achilles deserves more glory than Homer himself. Homer's poetic genius could sing of Achilles' deeds, and yet fully understand the shared pathology of the "heroic" Bronze Age (i.e., self-idealizing, violent, and insensitive). Rather, we would say that the place of the truly self-realized beings and true heroes has been usurped throughout history by patriarchal stars, who — in making their appearances — have exclaimed, in effect, "Adore me" (much like the devil in so many stories of medieval Christian folklore). Tótila Albert used to speak of the "Absolute Father" as an entity who possesses innumerable faces and expressions, and who demands — whether through the ecclesiastic or secular authorities of history (as well as through our Inner Father) — that we worship him, and thus cherish and obey his will.

Just as appreciative love can take place in a positive form or (in its inverse form) as a thirst for approval that we call narcissism, so erotic love can be distinguished in its positive form — as the will to give pleasure to others and oneself — and also by its passive or inverse form, the desire to be the object of the desire of others. When one knows only of the thirst for love, both things can be confused, for then this wish to be desired is called *love*. The distinction between these two reflects the difference between something that is part of our essential (instinctual) nature, and forms of what Maslow called "deficiency motivation," which involves seeking relief from a painful sense of emptiness. In the former case we can speak of *eros* proper; in the latter, it would be more fitting to use the Freudian term *libido*, since it is not the instinct of pleasure that dominates here, but rather a neurotic need to silence an experience of insignificance or loneliness.

Just as erotic love is usually degraded into the seductive offer of a sex object in patriarchal society, so *compassion* is mostly represented in ordinary life by a dutiful and shallow goodness, or — even worse — by a flagrant hypocrisy. What are we to make, for instance, of the fact that a dictator who destroyed many lives struck a Chilean journalist who interviewed him as "a good fellow with much love for his dog"? Such evaluations imply that in the absence of an actual experience of true compassion and benevolence, it is easy to allow oneself to be fooled by appearances. "He is a good fellow" can mean, in this case, "He performs his role, carrying out his duty as best he can"; or, "He does what he believes he must, and it is not that he isn't capable of loving."

Since false benevolence is a performance that is motivated by a need for approval, what appears to be maternal, empathetic, and compassionate love ultimately turns out to be a mask, which can easily get confused with a thirst for love and an expression of need, rather than protection and mothering.

In the world of the blind that we inhabit, this search for protection becomes mistaken (as in the dictator's good-natured appearance) for love in the true sense of the word. However, as self-awareness develops, such a person ends up discovering that what he had called "love" was, in reality, dependence — a prolongation of a childhood need into adult life; a neurotic bond that persisted because he did not receive enough love in his infancy, and which has, in turn, obstructed the unfolding of that generous and altruistic attitude in which a person may find his deeper satisfaction, once he has overcome his infantilism.

I began this chapter by proposing that the dominance of the father in the family and community at the dawning of our so-called civilized world created an imbalance between empathy and aggression in our collective life, and also led to the repression of the biological spontaneity of animal instinct. I then pointed out that the tyranny of the "father principle" has also affected human life by bringing about an idealization of the intellect at the expense of feelings and our empathetic "Mother principle," as well as the devaluation and inhibition of the innocent and sacred eros.

Next, I discussed things that, though easy to recognize, have not previously been placed at the center. I claimed that the essence of the patriarchal mind, with its hegemony of reason over love and healthy instinct, has disrupted the loving balance among our three inner persons. This has turned people into devitalized, cold-hearted beings — apparently devoted to their ideals, but in reality driven like machines by a patriarchal program that causes them to be compulsively accommodating, due to their dependence on affection and their vulnerability to punishment and rewards.

Thus, our emotional life — instead of being an "embrace of three" among our inner persons — is the outcome of a dysfunctional inner family. Here, the mammalian empathy that characterized our lives in the early Neolithic — along with the even more archaic organismic wisdom inherited from reptiles — languishes in an intra-psychic prison, where the jailer (who is also a judge and an accuser) wields a sword purporting to be dedicated to God's will, human justice, and the highest ideals. For the lie involved in the idealization of the patriarchal spirit makes us all into worshipers of golden calves.

Even *appreciative love* languishes, more and more, in our modern world. Increasingly, when flags are raised to proclaim freedom, democracy, or "values," this is done with dubious intentions. Increasingly, value ascription and reverent love have been degraded to the point where they are merely a mass of arguments and imperatives at the service of the greed or glory of unconsciously unhappy and predatory beings (although their greedy triumph may distract them from their emptiness and discontent).

However, in speaking of a generalized patriarchal mind that informs our culture, I do not mean to say that each individual is a kind of clone of a patriarchal prototype. Although an appreciable proportion of males exhibit what has been called a Tri-partite Model of Masculine Hegemony (TMMH)[2] (the aggression, domination, and insensitivity that are transmitted by means of their socialization), many women exhibit a contrasting syndrome, which has been called TMFH, for "Tripartite Model of Feminine Hegemony." Yet even the latter is part of the structure of patriarchal society and its corresponding mind. More generally, we can say that the Mother or Child within us have given in to the Absolute Father, even though (to a greater or lesser extent) they unconsciously rebel and resist his oppression in a dysfunctional manner.

But to continue with this train of thought would lead to an extensive treatise on the facets of universal neurosis, and for the time being, I feel satisfied to have shown that the center of patriarchy is the dominance of the Absolute Father, which our culture transmits like a plague. This coupling of domination-by-power with the exaltation of reason is used to justify and implement such dominance — not only over others, over nature, and over ourselves, but especially over our empathetic capacity and our instinctual life.

CHAPTER 6

THE ALTERNATIVE TO PATRIARCHY

There must be a strong desire to be just. There must be a growing capacity to be just. There must be discernment and sympathy in estimating the particular claims of divergent interests. There must be moral standards which discourage the quest for privilege and the exercise of arbitrary power. There must be resolution and valor, to resist oppression and tyranny. There must be patience and tolerance and kindness, in hearing claims and arguments in negotiation and reconciliation.

But these are human virtues. And though they are high, they are within the attainable limits of human nature, as we know it. They actually exist. Men do have these virtues — all but the most hopelessly degenerate — in some degree. We know that they can be increased. When we talk about them, we're talking about virtues that have affected the course of natural history, about virtues that some men have practiced more than other men. And no

man sufficiently, but enough men in great enough
degree to have given mankind, here and there, and
for varying periods of time, the intimations of a
good society.

— Walter Lippmann, "On Designing a New
Society," in *The Good Society*[1]

THE PROPHETS OF THE OLD Testament and the early Christians thought that we would one day come to live with one another in such a manner that there would be no other king on earth but God. A congruent view was the Gnostic conception of the *a-basileus*: those "without a king" who, having come into deep communion with Spirit, also attained a kingly status over themselves.

We may call the political character of such a vision "anarchy," in the all-too-forgotten sense of the word. For we tend to connote this term with dangerous chaos, correctly perceiving self-government as a threat to the established order. And yet there was no such fear of chaos in the minds of those who — less concerned with political repression — put their trust mostly in the relation of people with God. The idea that self-direction leads to self-organization rather than to chaos is also supported by psychological research and pedagogical experimentation, as is the belief that it is the curtailment of autonomy that leads to pathological consequences.

It needs to be said, however, that in the end, kingship was established in Israel, just as it had been established earlier in Egypt, Babylonia, and the rest of the nations. And it is also true that the interpreters of God (the prophets and the judges) — just as in the legendary day of the patriarchs, during the time of the Exodus and during the conquest of Palestine — had a degree of influence that made society definitely patriarchal, and not an illustration of that organismic condition which Lao Tze had conceived as a mythical antecedent to civilization, when he wrote in the *Tao Te Ching*: "When the original harmony was lost, laws arose."

The laws had long since arisen by the time Plato wrote *The Laws* and *The Republic*. And it is from him that we have been handed down what is perhaps the most beautiful defense of patriarchy that has ever been formulated. As is well known, he argues for a government by philosopher-kings: a council of the wise that would be especially educated — not only in knowledge, but also especially in virtue — to serve such a function.

Yet throughout history, government has been influenced by the thirst for power; and those seeking power have hardly been interested in giving too much of it to the service of virtue and truth. While it seems easy to *imagine* good government, it is not easy to actually *find* it, outside the realm of utopian thinking and fairy tales. In practice, throughout the history of civilization, obedience to the authority of government and laws has certainly not furthered the development of a life lived according to faith in the self-organizing activity of minds and communities.

At the same time, the power of patriarchy has become increasingly explosive. Precious as the work of Plato may be in the history of thought, we cannot say that it has been classical Greece's main contribution to politics. For the chief achievement of the Greeks, it is generally agreed, is that they invented democracy — or at least they *re-discovered* it some millennia after the dawn of patriarchal civilization in the late Neolithic.[2]

The Greeks had both the genius and the merit of daring to conceive of a "government of the people by the people," and of taking remarkable steps toward its realization. I think we judge the Athenians too superficially if — in saying that they still had slaves and looked down on women — we imply that, in our modern form of democracy, we have gone beyond such things. Perhaps we arrogantly deceive ourselves when we think this way: for patriarchy continues to be rampant, and it is far from evident that a world where governments serve the interests of profit-seeking modern corporations — while citizens are increasingly enslaved to work and salaries — constitutes a happier situation!

The Greeks had a true participatory democracy. The Athenians met in the agora to discuss public affairs; and, knowing each other personally, they confronted each other personally, too. In our democracy, however, we barely have the chance to express our political preferences every certain number of years, at the time of choosing one candidate or another among those who have reached such a status through money, propaganda, and promises that surely will remain unfulfilled. It is true that the sheer population of modern cities — to say nothing of modern nations — does not allow all the citizens to meet in person, and that if we want to restore a participatory democracy we need to think of doing so at a regional level (perhaps using modern information and communication technologies to help coordinate smaller democratic communities). Yet it is clear that the democratic ideal is far from having become a reality in the history of civilization, during which time the voice of the people — highly manipulated through education and the media — has constituted a rather weak counterbalance to the decisions of central power.

Not even Plato, who detested the ignorant democracy that condemned Socrates, came to think that his conception of a government by the wise could actually materialize, given the perversion of the world that surrounded him. Yet Socrates felt that it was meaningful to die for its sake, as a lesson for future generations and as a contribution to a future democracy, in whose potential he believed in spite of its blindness at that time.

Yet how different were the political ideals of the prophets and those of Greek society, with its extroversion and its conception of human beings as political animals!

Despite the existence of a chapter titled "The Birth of Greek Individualism" in Isaiah Berlin's book, *Liberty*,[3] the Greeks called the isolated individual an *idiot*. (Despite the modern negative connotation of this word, it originally had the precise meaning of a private individual.) Also, nothing could have been more remote from the Greek mentality than the idea that people had the right to do whatever they felt like. Indeed, Aristotle taught against thinking that an individual belongs to himself (or herself). According to him, all people belonged to the Polis. And Pericles believed that a person who governs is proud of his people in the same way that a headmaster is proud of his school, or a commander is proud of his army. Athens was a society in which no compulsion was necessary, for it could be said that its citizens acted out of spontaneous loyalty, in devotion to their people. There cannot be a question, then, that the *inner* dimension of democracy implied by such statements is something that we are very far from embodying today, in spite of our enthusiastic democratic rhetoric.

However, independently of how little democracy may have progressed in the world since the time of the Greeks, since then the democratic dream was implanted in our patriarchal world. Perhaps its realization was never so near as in the Florentine city-state in the time of Dante, at a time when the nobility had lost most of its privileges. (Dante Alighieri — a pharmacist, according to his guild — was one of the seventy "priors" then governing the city, and its ambassador to the Pope, from whose prison he fortunately — both for him and us — managed to escape.)

Political reality is one thing, however, and the reality of books another. We hardly find any democracy in Dante's book *De Monarchia*, which was revolutionary enough to be burnt in the public square, yet nevertheless presented an ideal that (in spite of the scandal that it provoked) was purely patriarchal: a mere symmetry in power between the Church and the State, which is to say between the Pope and the Emperor.

This happened a long time after the church had unquestionably dominated society. A slow reawakening of the secular world was beginning, along with a rediscovery of the Greco-Roman legacy. Against this background, the ideal of the republic began to be forged by minds like Machiavelli's. And when Luther, denouncing papal corruption, lent the nobility even greater power in relation to the church, he gave further momentum to a liberation movement that culminated in the Enlightenment, along with the French Revolution, Cromwell's accession to power, and the independence of the American colonies.

If we seek the dream behind the pioneering revolution of the French, we find it not so much in the rationalism of Kant, Voltaire, and the Encyclopedists as in the mind of Rousseau. More a romantic than a rationalist, more an engaged human being than an academic, Rousseau's grave in Paris has been visited throughout the centuries by people who have regarded him as a saint-like being for his wisdom and love of humankind. Like Freud after him, Rousseau saw the dysfunctional and oppressive structure of society; yet he had more trust than Freud in freedom, in nature, in education, and in the community's collaboration toward the common good.

We may say that in the age of Beethoven, Romanticism, and the French Revolution, the political dream was one of brotherhood as well as freedom; one in which solidarity and equity would go hand in hand with a faith in democratic government. And thus we may say that the old prophetic dream of freedom from authority and the Greek dream of solidarity were now fused into one.

Of course, the Greeks were more successful in their experiments with democracy than were the French in the days of the Terror, or later under Napoleon. Still, the dream was one of concern for the common good, and it foreshadowed the French pioneering commune centered around the figure of Proudhon, whose ideas in turn inspired Marx and some of the anarchists of the nineteenth century.

Before that, however, the dream found a better fate in America, when the fathers of the new nation — after forging their independence from England — came together to conceive the creation of a new society. We could say (at least implicitly) that in their conception, a sense of concern for the common good coincided with a keen appreciation of the pursuit of freedom in a vision that did not exclude the patriarchal principle of authority.

The formulation of the United States Constitution was influenced not only by Locke's liberalism and that of English legislation, but also by the less explicit example of the American Indians. For their tribal government was more admired by Thomas Jefferson, Benjamin Franklin, and others than the history of the relations between white-skinned and red-skinned Americans may have led us to imagine. Even more significant than the U.S. Constitution in the history of the new political vision was the document that the authors of the Federalist Papers — Hamilton, Madison, and Adams — produced, in their

effort to win the support of New Yorkers. It was the best utopia that patriarchy had yet formulated. Nor was it a *purely* patriarchal vision, as Plato's had been; for it incorporated not only
the ideals of rule by law and the preventive balance of power
through its division into executive, legislative, and judiciary
branches of government (already proposed by Montesquieu),
but also the previous dreams of community and of safeguard-
ing individual freedoms.

Yet today, it is painfully evident that not even an excellent
constitution is a guarantee of justice or success in the collective pursuit of happiness. I think it admirable that even this
limitation was lucidly envisioned by the authors of the Federalist Papers; for they made explicit their understanding that the
conception of rule-by-law could only work for a virtuous community
(which, for them, meant Christian).

I don't think I need to argue for the statement of the obvious in saying that our modern world is far from even *valuing*
virtue (except for image building and its political advantages).
History has proven the founding fathers right: corruption,
violence, injustice, exploitation, indifference to the common
good, and selfishness cannot be curbed by laws or police alone,
nor inculcated by those who only pay lip service to them without embodying "the further reaches of human nature," to use
Maslow's felicitous expression. Thus, if a government were serious about the common good, it could not fail to educate its
citizenry toward goodness — and not just for the sake of accu-
mulating scientific information, conformity, or wealth.

Today, most societies are multi-cultural and increasingly
secular, and no one religion can be expected to guarantee the
generalized virtue of a people. Yet nothing has been more neglected than the kind of education for virtue that Plato conceived as the highest aspiration of government (and for which

moralizing, preaching, or lecturing on values are no substitute).

Needless to say, the American Constitution was flawed enough to allow for slavery, male chauvinism and, more recently, the scape-goating of the poor. Therefore, we should beware of turning it into another "sacred book" or into a magical solution to our problems. I say this not merely because it could only work in a virtuous context, as it was understood from the beginning. It is also because the Industrial Age, since its beginnings — when Henry VIII confiscated the monasteries for the sake of his barons, and the bourgeoisie was taken over in the days of the French and Colonial revolutions — has become increasingly violent, technologically exploitive, and ignorant. In spite of the many universities and the progress of science and technology, the Industrial Age has needed Marx's criticism, just as the individual mind has needed its Freud.

For Marx, the main issue was that the Good Society *not* have a government. He foresaw that, with the transcendence of private property, money could also come to disappear. As we shifted towards that ideal world, he proposed, the economy would be geared first (under socialism) to provide for each human being according to his capacity, and later (under communism) to each according to his or her needs. We all know how he believed that in order to achieve a communist society, it would first be necessary to go through a transitional "dictatorship of the proletariat"; and we all know what a beastly *cul-de-sac* that came to be, in spite of his optimistic dream. For, curiously, Marx did not seem to have expected proletarians to be susceptible to the corruption of power. It is a pity that, today, the failure of the brigands who spoke in his name reflects negatively on Marx himself, just as other brigands who have spoken for Christ have in the end brought Christianity into disrepute and seeming irrelevance.

If we compare the political ideals of the American Founding Fathers with those of Marx, we may say that the former sought to integrate mostly patriarchal or central government into democracy — through parliamentary representation and elections — while the latter sought the convergence of democracy (as the very word *communism* conveys) and anarchy. Furthermore, Lenin's attempt to embody the revolution conveyed a double message: although dictatorship was proclaimed hateful, it was simultaneously embraced with the same zest with which it was denounced — but deceptively, and under the guise of rationalizations.

Hegel proposed that history advances through the development of ideas in the minds of exceptional people. Yet in the history of Marxism, we might say that it was the *personalities* of Marx, Lenin, and Stalin that explain both the violent antagonism to the authority principle and the expectation that despotism might be overcome through despotism. Let us bear in mind, by the way, that already in Marx's day, despotism — unlike in earlier times of patriarchy — was not mainly that of State and Church, but rather manifested as the enslavement of labor by money-holders. And since many people have realized the extent to which capitalism — an exploitive, unfair, and (despite appearances) most unbrotherly and unholy economy — has been embraced by governments, the world has not quite been the same.

Understandable as it may be that vindictive leaders may have underestimated the place of government in human affairs, let us return to the theme of the Good Society — and to my statement that the U.S. had a valid vision in its intent to bring together central authority, communal authority, and the authority of the individual. I propose that *just as hierarchical power is the essence of patriarchy, and tribal power (or "government*

*by the people") is matristic politics, so anarchy (or self-empowerment)
and self-government are the political mode of our "Inner Child."*

Of all the above, however, we may say that there is a
wholesome and valid form of expression, and also a degraded
form. So the hierarchy arising from the influence of wisdom
deteriorates when under the corrupt authority of power seekers;
the voice of community can become the blind power of the
mob or manipulated conformity; and the freedom of the sane
individual may degenerate into the aggressive individualism of
egoism, in the absence of emotional health.

We could say, as well, that the Child aspect of human
nature was implicitly degraded in the bourgeois republican
ideal, where "rugged individualism" — divorced from solidarity
— was becoming crypto-cannibalistic; and that Marx and the
anarchists were unwittingly seeking to do it justice. Yet their
rebellious opposition to government (or, at least, the opposition
of their followers) was not healthy enough to succeed; for it
was not supported by true trust in humanity. Thus, we should
not wonder that an anti-despotic ideology would later become
even more despotic than the czarist regime that had kindled
its opposition.

Continuing in our story of utopias, I want to consider
one that is not nearly as articulate as those described thus far,
which might be better described as a collective intuition than
a model of the Good Society. Flourishing during the 1960s
and '70s, it could be called "the spirit of the New Age," "the
vision of the counter-culture," or, perhaps, "the psychedelic
utopia." Although it fell short of being a rationally articulated
political model, still it threatened the patriarchal world with
a revolution perceived as dangerous enough to stir the coun-
ter-revolution of neo-conservatism — along with (according to
social linguist George Lakoff) its attendant fear of freedom,

preoccupation with the danger of drugs, moralism, and the "severe father" model of political life.

It was aptly summarized by Tim Leary's injunction to "turn on, tune in, and drop out" — in which "tuning in" referred to inwardness, mystical mindedness, and openness to intuition, while "dropping out" stood for the quintessence of the counter-culture: a choice of detachment rather than rebellion, and a will to leave the madness of civilized life behind, becoming sort of nomadic wanderers or participants in a social experiment of unconventional community life.*

The social criticism inspired by the "consciousness revolution" (as it was then called) manifested in many ways, ranging from a pacifist opposition to the Vietnam War and a concern for justice and civil liberties, to feminism and ecology. Mostly, however, such criticism stemmed from a pervasive and intuitive sense of the sickness and aberration of conventional culture — arrived at not through reflection but from the vantage point of psychedelic consciousness.

Just as existentialism had put life before theory, so the spirit of the New Age cared little for ideology, and much for experience and intuition as a compass in the adventure of "doing one's own thing." There was an Emersonian self-reliance to it,[4] and much mysticism — without the language of traditional religion, in spite of a generalized interest in the Eastern spiritual traditions. One could read "Hail to the One Cosmic Mind" at the entrance of Shambhala Bookstore in Berkeley, for instance; and the ideas of the Tao and karma became part of the common language of the youth. Mostly, however, the

---

* Turning on, of course, referred to the use of psychedelics in order to access the inner vision and love out of which both the healthy community might be born and the old "Establishment" abandoned.

zeitgeist was shamanic; and it is no wonder that it was a sha-
man who became the star among best-selling authors: Carlos
Castaneda.

To say that the spirit of the age was shamanic implies that
it was also Dionysian, as was observed by theologian Sam Keen
in his book, *To a Dancing God*. Victorianism was over, already
unmasked long ago by Freud and Nietzsche; and the cure of
the day was the undoing of repression through spontaneity,
expression, and surrender to life, with the inspiration of inner
guidance.

Parents, however, were not so happy about this; and there
was much talk about the increased gap between the generations. Parental anger supported repressive politicians, who
scapegoated the youth just as Hitler had done with the Jews,
ridiculed the New Age, and criminalized marijuana, the "food
of the gods."*

It is too bad that psychedelics became illegal, forbidden
even to psychotherapy and religion. For it seems criminal to
dispense with their remarkable healing potential when we so
much need both healing and a better spiritual perspective. Yet
those in power became afraid of too much democracy and inner freedom; and today's new conservatism, with its attempt
to seize repressive control, is the mirror image of the New Age.
Constructed to be its perfect opposite, it secretly entertains a
war against consciousness expansion — and not only of the psychedelic variety, but even through education (as the irrelevancy
of education to human development tragically shows). Today's
new conservatives have managed to secularize the world fur-

---

* Just as Teonanacatl ("food of the gods") was the Mexican word for the
"sacred mushroom," many today speak of "entheogens"—i.e., substances
that generate the experience of the divine—rather than hallucinogens or
psychedelics.

ther away from spirit than ever, in order to ward off the danger of any independent faith that might lend support to a challenge of the neo-liberal creed;* and to make things even worse, they have contributed to a generalized distaste for ideals of any kind. Academics (who are not necessarily courageous, and who live on the pay of conservatively supported universities) are of no help, in our post-modern days; for they tell us that all values are relative, and that what we used to call "great ideas" now need to be deconstructed.

Yet we need a vision that may take us beyond the mercantile-patriarchal model, particularly since it is not clear that the answer can lie in the feminist notion of a simple return to the matristic spirit, or in a simple "government of the people by the people."

In such times, maybe we could find inspiration in Tótila Albert, who not only turned against the despotism of civil and religious authority and insisted on the political potential of self-government, but also emphasized the primacy of that healthy and virtuous condition at whose core he envisioned the "harmony of the three" in both the biological and the intra-psychic family.

If the implicit political model of filiarchy was anarchy or autarchy; if the model of matristic politics was tribal, or community centered; and if the model of patriarchy is dictatorial power in the family and in society; then, Tótila Albert contended, these three possible forms of unbalanced life might one day come to be replaced by a *balance of the three* — a triadic integration — not only in the individual but also in society,

---

* Different as the words "neo-conservative" and "neo-liberal" may sound, the reality behind them is the affirmation of the self-same "spirit of modern capitalism," whose most important freedoms are those of buying and, most especially, selling.

once this balance may be supported by a new development in individual consciousness. As will be seen, it is my contention that the wholesomeness of individual consciousness could be achieved in the span of a single generation, if only the world community understood the political relevance of a massive and radical educational reform, so that instead of using public education for patriarchal indoctrination, governments decided to use it for human growth and social evolution.

This transition from the patriarchal regime to the regime of triadic integration would be, then, a transition from hierarchy to heterarchy[5] — a condition in which central authority would not be replaced but instead counterbalanced by the will of both the community and the individual.

While each of the political models known in history, it is clear, has degenerated — so that anarchy became a cannibalistic thrust for the "survival of the fittest"; democracy, a paralyzing group tyranny; and the patriarchal spirit, an inhuman and blind despotism — we may still harbor the hope that an integration among the three possible political alternatives that we have known throughout history may protect us from such excesses, much like what was originally expected from separating the legislative, judicial, and executive powers in government.

Though the writers of the American Constitution may be said to have already conceived, out of common sense, a synthesis among the ideals of central government, democracy, and a healthy individualism, it is clear that contemporary political reality is far from embodying such a conception. It seems to me that two fundamental things have been missing. The first is putting the *healthy balance of the individual mind* at the center of politics. And the second is "educationalism,"[6] a term coined by Brazilian senator Cristovam Buarque to describe the ideology that sees education as the heart of social revolution and as the best path (after the failures of neo-liberalism and socialism, alike) to the "utopia" of a sustainable world — with freedom and without the "golden wall" of a new apartheid between the rich and the poor.

Of course, Amartya Sen and Bernardo Kliksberg[7] also are right when they see the reintegration of ethics into the economy as the central issue of humanity's way ahead. However, we will need to make a distinction between *extrinsic* or *normative* ethics and an ethics that has its foundation in *virtue*, a quality of the mind akin to mental health. For it is easy to agree with Lao Tze to the effect that normative or authoritarian ethics (based on what George Lakoff calls the "severe father model") arose "when the original harmony was lost." What we need, then, and what this book proposes, is the transformation of education to produce whole and wholesome "three-brained beings" — who, in turn may be suited to realize the heterarchic political ideal described above.

The world today is scarcely democratic, despite the neoconservative rhetoric that identifies democracy with free enterprise and serves principally to hide its claws. Not even influential politicians who carry the banner of democracy truly believe in what they say. Yet it is easy to understand their reticence; for since the dawn of civilized life, true democracy has never been tried. And despite appearances that our present democracy gives ample space to individualism, this individualism is available only to a population that has been systematically robotized, to the point of losing contact with their genuine desires, emotions, and even independent thinking. The typical expression of this individualism is greed, which (since the well-intentioned Adam Smith) we have ennobled with the word "interest" and postulated as the main motive in human life.

What to do, then?

When the Russians discovered Gurdjieff, before the days of Bolshevism, to be a human being of exceptional wisdom, they used to ask him this question: "What to do?" And he used to reply that such a question had no meaning in the mouth of automatons: for in order to be able to *do*, it is first necessary to *be*; and only after knowing itself can a machine go beyond being a simple machine.

At that time, the question interested only a few individuals, who were especially endowed for the great spiritual adventure. Today, however, when it becomes apparent that we cannot have a sane society without extensive individual wholesomeness, it concerns us all.

CHAPTER 7

A TRI-FOCAL EDUCATION TO TRANSCEND PATRIARCHY

There is an obvious tension between schools as machines for the production of competitive skilled workers and schools as learning communities for the creation of citizens.

How effective will our economy be if it depends on a generation of listless, anxious people, unable to concentrate on anything very long, and unconcerned about planning a coherent life for themselves? There is literally nothing more important than the quality of our young people. Yet American public policy consistently refuses to pay attention to this fact.

— Robert Bellah, *The Good Society*

WHAT CAN BE DONE?

IF, AS I HAVE PROPOSED, THE crux of our *problematique* is a "fall," or degradation of consciousness, that occurred at the dawn of civilization — which entailed the loss of the wholeness of our mind as a result of an insane hegemony of our rational brain at the expense of our empathetic capacity and our organismic or instinctive wisdom — then it follows that nothing could be as important as healing individual consciousness on a widespread scale: in other words, *fostering the massive psycho-spiritual development of the population.*

It is true that the patriarchal mind develops from the impingement of many factors, ranging from birth trauma and inadequate mother-child bonding to a punitive environment and sexual repression. However, once its essence is recognized as an experiential impoverishment due to the loss of compassion and inner freedom, it would be most desirable for international organizations and governments to recognize the importance of providing a remedial attention to a psycho-spiritual development that has not been properly nurtured — and indeed, that has been increasingly choked, in our time, by the escalating degree to which parents are consumed by the struggle to survive and by an increasingly enslaving market. In view of this modern phenomenon, an awareness of the importance of inner growth and healing would inspire a hypothetically wise and free government to provide sufficient time for its citizens, free from the compulsion to earn a living "by the sweat of one's brow" — "sabbatical" time in which to simply be, grow, and share. Yet in a system that increasingly subordinates life to profit and subjects all values to cost/benefit analysis, we can imagine how unproductive such a proposition would sound to the bureaucrats, managers, and politicians.

And then there are other problems. One is that in the case of most adults, the "metaphysical thirst" that is so natural in children and young adolescents has already been put to sleep. Furthermore, the culture has interpreted the natural yearning for growth as a mere search for love, prestige, or security – things that are not only desired but also socially validated, so that they seem easier to attain than spiritual fulfillment. Not only does leisure time fail to be perceived as a great opportunity to those in whose spirit the quest for something that lies beyond the culturally transmitted values has become dormant or withered, but it is perceived as a torture. Blaise Pascal observed, centuries ago, that "the sole cause of man's unhappiness is that he does not know how to stay quietly in his room"[1] – and today, more than ever, people's inability to be at peace with themselves and to savor their existence by "staying quietly in their room" generates individual and social problems. People no longer *know* what to do with their freedom, and they work hard to spend a good part of their free time and their money on distractions or entertainment, which lend themselves admirably to distancing them from becoming aware of what they really feel and think.

Aside from the fact that very few people seek the "goodness of their soul," there is also the problem of those who claim to offer them help. As Ivan Illich so keenly observed, as soon as a need creates a great market, the interests of the market prevail over those of the people. When hospitals arose, charity, he claims, diminished; when construction companies emerged, people were discouraged from building their own houses. Comparably, when churches offered help to those seeking contact with the Divine, the result often became complicated, subverted, or contaminated in response to the churches' political agendas and implicit authoritarianism.

Something similar occurs with institutionalized public health care. Like religion, this arose from a very good intention; but it has suffered from the patriarchal contamination of a system whose ends it serves, above and beyond those of its clients. We well know that public health care hardly recognizes the *psychological* aspects of diseases, preferring prescription drugs (thus serving the interests of laboratories) to psychotherapy, and that its understanding of mental health is more a matter of adaptation to society than of an individual's adaptation to his or her own nature, or to life.

Even more problematic than all this, however, is the fact that in the Great Journey of the Soul, many more are "called" than "chosen." For even with sufficient motivation, time, and money, few succeed in finding inner peace and happiness. Healing — which comes from reaching a degree of human development that involves insight, sensitivity to beauty, and a spontaneous orientation towards goodness — generally requires a heroic uphill journey that few manage to carry out. Much easier than *healing* our psycho-spiritual ills, then, is *preventing* them.

Because of this — and because both spiritual traditions and psychotherapy are slow, expensive, and likely to serve only a few — I believe that, at our present moment in history, *education* may provide greater salvific potential. At least, it *could* be of more use to us if we decided to put it at our service.

For it is a tragic fact that education — the institution that is supposedly *responsible* for human development — has not only neglected psycho-spiritual growth, but has even come to be entirely at the service of preserving the status quo and socializing the young into the patriarchal mind. And future teachers — despite the long years of schooling that they are required to spend in the academic world — undergo a professional training that seems perfectly designed as a conditioning process to make them forget what true education might be. So successful is this conditioning that the repetitive and dehumanizing labor which is expected from them in the end seems to them simply "normal."

Yet it is not easy for teachers to ignore altogether the meaninglessness of the profession that the dictates of institutional inertia and political preferences demand. Surely, it is not only the low pay and lack of appreciation from students that explain their many psychosomatic ailments and generalized depression; it is also the lack of true meaning in what they do with their time and life.

The first thing that needs to be done, then, is to transform education so that it becomes transformative.

MORE EDUCATION?

Now and then, I meet people who think the world would be better if we had more education; and we all know of charitable institutions that take this assumption for granted. Therefore, before setting out to share my vision of what constitutes a desirable education, I think it appropriate to preface this by saying that I do not agree.

I do not think it would help us to have more of what we, today, call "education." Instead, I sympathize with parents who choose to take their children out of school to guide them – or let them guide themselves – through a learning process at home (and, more broadly, beyond even the confines of the schools or learning centers).

I also sympathize with the idea of deschooling put forth by Ivan Illich. However, since we already have schools, I think that it would be best to use them for something truly meaningful. And since we have created a legislation that imposes mandatory education, this could give us the opportunity to switch from a mandatory patriarchal socialization to an education for

wholeness — one that emphasizes human development, freedom, and a healthy social evolution.

The older I get, the more clearly I see things, and the
more convinced I am that we have the world we have because
we do not have an education that is more relevant to our real
needs.

The educational model prevailing today grew out of the
early Industrial Age. It is largely oriented toward a curriculum
that implicitly teaches people to respect their superiors, keep
quiet, and be patient with repetitive tasks. But what we need,
more and more urgently, is education that fosters the development of people's whole minds — not just intellectually, but
also in regard to competencies involving the sensory, motor,
emotional, communicative, imaginative, aesthetic, and spiritual
realms.

What we have today is mainly an education that perpetu-
ates the social system — a reproductive organ of collective consciousness that operates from an implicit assumption that we
live in the best of all possible worlds, and that it is desirable to
perpetuate our ways of being, thinking, and living. Yet we must
realize that our innumerable social problems — which have
taken us to what looks like the edge of an abyss — are related
to our psycho-spiritual underdevelopment, and that we have
the world we have because of our own limitations. And once
we realize that, we must conclude that traditional education is
at the very heart of our many-faceted world problem.

My vocation has been that of helping people grow; and my
everyday work has shown me how even those people who feel

moved to seek wider horizons than those of the ordinary citizen suffer the consequences of having remained emotionally under-developed, alienated from their true selves and deeper consciousness. Dazzled by the rhetoric of progress, we do not realize how much our affective life is impoverished in the modern world. Nor do we realize that — at the same time that the world is enriched with the discoveries of science and technology — most people are becoming impoverished, not only in terms of economics but also in terms of their quality of life. Yet although education has served the goal of making us as much like our ancestors as possible, through socialization, domestication of the mind, and indoctrination, we may imagine that it may some day reformulate its goals and come to place development above the status quo.

In the *Mahabharata* — the great epic that, for ancient India, was a treasure of wisdom, comparable to what Homer's epic poems were to the Greco-Roman world — the plot revolves around a great war that the ancients regarded as the beginning of our fallen age (the Iron Age, or Kali Yuga). The narrative explains the origin of the two warring sides of the Mahabharata — the virtuous Pandavas and their enemies, the Kauravas — in the following way:

The Kauravas are the children of a blind king, whose wife lovingly chooses to blindfold herself so that she will not outshine her husband. In her self-abnegation, she makes a wish for her children to be like him; and as a result of this "loving wish," she gives birth to a metal ball — from which, in turn, originate her one hundred problematic sons. The king who is the ancestor of the epic's virtuous Pandavas, on the other hand (and whose name, Pandu, alludes to the color white), is not exactly their father, as in the story of Joseph in the Christian Gospel: King Pandu's two wives are visited and impregnated by different gods, and his children — reflections of the heavenly entities whom the wives have invoked — are born heroic, or semi-divine.

When we talk politics, we are not given to myths and fairy tales. And yet I believe that this old poem describes — better than abstract language — the basic alternative we need to bear in mind in the area of education. Wanting "more of the same" seems noble and patriotic, and we do not hesitate to consider it an expression of our love. But are we not undergoing a crisis of obsolescence, in which the persistence of the patriarchal spirit that has been with us since the beginning of civilization has become potentially deadly? Rather than continuing to want more of the same thing, then, it would be better to do something like those women who called on the gods in their aspiration towards something different and higher than what had been known until then.

Once we understand that the answer to our innumerable ills is no longer within the reach of politics — that our hope lies in elevating, deepening, or expanding people's consciousness on a mass scale — then we need to understand that what we currently have is not only a patriarchal *society*, but also a patriarchal *educational system*. We need to understand that what we call "education," today, is nothing more than instruction: an activity whose primary concern is the transmission of information that fails to be essentially concerned with understanding, to say nothing of wisdom.

Of course, a comprehensive educational curriculum should include an interpersonal or affective aspect. And UNESCO's much-cited declaration — to the effect that it should attend not only to "learning to do" but also to "learning to learn," "learning to live among others," and "learning to be" — takes this into account. Furthermore, in light of what I have already said regarding what it would mean to educate for wholeness, a comprehensive educational curriculum should include the re-integration of the mind's *instinctual* aspect, to heal the repressive attitude that has been intrinsic to patriarchal culture since the beginnings of civilized life. In other words, education should not only be concerned with people's ability to think and to develop healthy affective ties with one another, but should also cultivate freedom, and take an interest in the *happiness* of the learners.

And should not an education for wholeness also be concerned with that deeper aspect of the mind on which the meaning of life and the harmony of our inner parts depend? It is to this deeper mind — distinct from the intellect and even from ideals — which traditionally has been called "spirit," that UNESCO has drawn attention in contending that it is important not only to learn to do, to learn, and to live together, but also to *be*.

In the rest of this chapter, I will elaborate further on what education could be, once harnessed to the task of making us into better human beings, and thus also serving the evolution of society. In my earlier approach to this subject, in "Educating the Whole Person for the Whole World,"[2] I updated Aldous Huxley's review in "The Education of an Amphibian" of the wealth of resources that, in view of our multifaceted mind, could be integrated into an education for wholeness. Now, I will concentrate mainly on the aspects that today's educational system has neglected, in spite of a widespread rhetoric endorsing the cultivation of "values":

- Experiential knowledge of one's own mind.
- The relational and the social, which are closely related to our "inner mothering" competences.

- The emancipatory aspect, which entails freeing the "Inner Child" within each of us.
- The spiritual aspect of education.

COGNITIVE GAPS

THE QUESTION of the learning that education should take into account has been approached so lucidly by Edgar Morin[3] that I will say little here on the subject, apart from pointing out that understanding is much more important than mere information, and wisdom much more valuable than mere knowledge. However, I do want to endorse Morin's recommendation that — in addition to emphasizing complexity, the trans-disciplinary perspective, and the need to concentrate on essentials — we direct our yearning for truth towards the *inner* world, not only towards the knowledge of outer things.

Our "traditional education" has been remarkably blind to the wisdom of Socrates (as is civilization itself, for allowing it). This master of philosophers, who was perhaps the greatest teacher in Western history, not only embodied the wisdom of acknowledging one's own ignorance and excelled in the art of maieutic dialogue,* but also led his life according to the mandate, "know thyself" (inscribed over the entrance to the temple of Apollo by the Delphic oracle). We have built a great monument to Socrates in the cosmopolitan city of our modern mind; but until now, we have failed to do him the honor of heeding his advice. For an education that is limited to knowledge of the outer world alone can be rich only on the surface. And

----

* A term related to midwifery, which came to be applied to someone who uses words to aid the psychic birth of others.

the absence of attention to cultivating knowledge of the inner world would seem to have resulted from the complicity between education and a politico-economic system that works best when served by robotized, easily manipulated human beings.

Knowing oneself is not a matter of studying psychology. It is a matter of life experience rather than of thought. It begins with awareness of our feelings and perceptions, progresses toward the recognition of our emotions, includes the subtle consciousness of the thought process, and can attain a transpersonal level that transcends the spheres of thinking, feeling, and even doing. Prompted by a thirst for transcendence or truth, the call to know oneself becomes a quest — until, like Oedipus, the individual comes to solve the sphinx's enigma.

The oft-repeated oracular motto, "know thyself," encompasses two meanings. One, psychological, refers to the knowledge of our own personal experiences, and the understanding of our personality, our unconscious motivations, our relationships with others, and our lives. Another — which we may call "spiritual," "transpersonal," "philosophical," or "mystical" — is directed towards understanding our deeper nature: a consciousness that we usually call "I," and which constitutes an identity that is deeper than the roles and traits making up our psychological identity, and that escapes conceptual definition.

In an educational undertaking, both aspects of self-knowledge are relevant. Yet both of them are notably missing from our institutionalized education.

Just as the ancients distinguished between the goal of the minor mysteries (oriented toward the "true man") and the major mysteries (whose aim was the "whole" or "universal" man), is it not time for the mandatory education offered by modern states to contemplate including in its curricula both a laboratory of emotional awareness (the first step towards a healing process) and an experiential exploration of the contemplative dimension of the mind?

I will come back later to the subject of spiritual education. But before closing this commentary on the need for education to expand its cognitive horizons, I want to point out that such an expansion will necessarily require an "ethics of economy," in regard to what may be the essential elements of our future scientific and humanistic education. For if we want future curricula to include an experiential education — aiming at such things as self-knowledge, kindness, freedom, and subtle, non-attached attention — then we will have to make room for such things. It is certainly not desirable to badger students with meaningless knowledge, nor to drown them in information, much as the "brave new world" prophetically described by Aldous Huxley drowned people in amusement, advertising, and drugs.

TOWARDS A PEDAGOGY OF LOVE

IF WE take seriously UNESCO's recommendation of ensuring that people learn to live together (among other things), we need to be aware that this will not happen spontaneously, through group or community interactions alone. Living together also requires the intention to heal our emotional world, which underlies our relationships with others as well as with ourselves. And healing our *emotional* world entails recovering our natural capacity to love — which in turn involves unlearning, or detaching from, those destructive attitudinal patterns that we acquired in childhood in reaction to unfortunate circumstances and to the psychological difficulties of family members.

Since I have described my work on the recovery of love elsewhere,[4] I will address the subject here in its broad outlines, and begin by saying that much is possible — as long as we know how to combine certain little-known powerful resources. To begin with, affective education cannot be conceived of as being separate from the experiential process of self-knowledge, which may also be regarded as the heart of psychotherapy. Such self-knowledge process involves a sort of "descent into hell": a purification through which the dysfunctional aspects of emotional life are acknowledged and gradually deactivated through understanding.

But self-knowledge is not everything. There must also be a *catharsis* of repressed childhood emotions, and these must not only be recalled but also fully re-experienced by diving deeply into them. In addition, it is necessary to *unlearn* the automatic or habitual behavior patterns through which we express our "negative emotions."

There are plenty of resources available for educating the heart in the fields of psychotherapy and spirituality, as I have already mentioned in other books.[5] Yet I think that our ideal should not be merely to import such resources into our schools, but rather to achieve a more complex assimilation: a new synthesis. We need something akin to a "technology transfer" from the fields of therapy and spirituality into education, anchored in sufficient experiential understanding to be able to dispense with the terminology and standard formulas of either psychotherapy or religion.

The following example, taken from a book in which Rebecca Wild talks about her Pestalozzi school near Quito, Ecuador, may convey how the therapeutic endeavor requires neither the form nor the language of psychotherapy, but depends rather on a certain kind of understanding and the appropriate attitude:

There was a little girl — small, chubby and very pampered — who did nothing in kindergarten for three months but sweep, scrub floors and wash dishes. One day her very distinguished, elegant father, with a very serious expression on his face, asked me, "Could you tell me what you've done with my daughter here?"

I had little experience and felt unsure — cornered, you might say — and I tried to give the gentleman a lesson in the Montessori method. But he shook his head and said he wasn't interested in that.

"You see," he explained, "before my daughter came here she didn't care about me at all, and now she loves me. I just wanted to know how you did it."[6]

As this illustration suggests, the true basis for making such an educational action possible will not be techniques or a revised curriculum. Rather, it will be a combination of a political will that makes affective education a priority, and an experiential understanding of emotional life and emotional healing on the part of future teachers. And for this to happen, they will need the opportunity to acquire therapeutic and spiritual insight through first-hand experience in such areas. We may hope that those who dictate educational policies also see fit to bring an experiential laboratory into the school curricula, one that is specifically aimed at fostering a more benevolent, appreciative, and joyful generation than ours. I use these three words — "benevolent," "appreciative," and "joyful" — in reference to the three facets of love, which (as I have suggested throughout this book) correspond to the maternal-empathic aspect of our psyche, to the paternal or value-ascribing, and to our "Inner Child."

If those who teach could clearly understand that happiness depends on the expression of our potential for loving, and that the ability to love is the best guarantee against the insatiable thirst for love that characterizes our degraded condition of consciousness, they would surely transmit this conviction. In the process, they would do their students a great favor by getting them interested in the idea that love is something that can be *cultivated*, through a combination of self-awareness concerning the inner aspect of love problems, and practice. Self-awareness is indispensable to "the path of love"; for even the best intentions concerning the cultivation of love are met with inner obstacles so powerful that even the "religion of love" that has inspired Western civilization has not sufficed to move us beyond polite barbarism. These inner obstacles to love, sometimes called "negative" or "destructive emotions," are none other than those that early Christianity designated as the "cardinal sins": pride, envy, anger, and so on. In Hindu spirituality (which tends to be less criminalizing than Christian culture), these are simply called "hindrances"; and Oscar Ichazo, in his "protoanalysis," called them "passions." I think that a still more precise expression, in our day, would be "forms of deficiency motivation."

The old doctrine of purification, or liberation of a soul that is chained by its sins, is no different from the modern notion of liberation of the true self from its neurotic needs. Yet both the language of sin and that of pathology are foreign to the current vocabulary of education, which is dominated by constructivism and behaviorism; and the dual taboo concerning therapeutic and religious concepts may pose a serious obstacle to a truly effective pedagogy of love. For without a language by which to address our "mental parasites" — whether they are called "sins" or "neurotic needs" — we are at the mercy of our defects.

The resistance of educators to psychotherapy is understandable, given the premature and exaggerated pretensions of psychoanalysis put forth some decades ago. As for their resistance to religion, this is also understandable as an unpleasant aftertaste of their reaction to the past hegemonic tendencies of the churches. However, in the same way that religion and spiritual development are different things, so is the therapeutic domain one thing and the institution of professional psychotherapy another.

Any therapy, particularly since Freud, involves understanding one's past and plunging again into certain past experiences such as grief, aggression, and frustrated desires. Why should education, then, in its own way not be able to do the same — particularly in view of the well-known fact that the children who come into the schools are increasingly disturbed?

Healing from the emotional wounds of the past involves not only remembering, understanding, and experiencing a catharsis, but also a process of making peace with the past. This reconciliation, in turn, entails understanding, compassion, and forgiveness. This is something that psychoanalysis discovered but rarely achieves. Yet if we want education to acquire something of the healing function exercised by psychotherapy thus far, I am sure we have the necessary resources to uncover wounded love, understand its scars, and help people detach from obsolete dysfunctional responses.

Both self-knowledge and detachment are psychological processes that the ancients must have understood well, for they ascribed them to the god Apollo. This makes sense: Apollo is the god of both self-awareness and harmony, and we can say that self-knowledge *leads* to harmony. In his myth, Apollo is represented as an archer, whose precise and deadly arrows (which are like a prolongation of his precise gaze) defeat monsters; and we may say that these arrows are a symbol for impartial awareness. Does not awareness of the truth free us of our inner monsters more effectively than force?

But the liberating consciousness of truth does not come about only through self-observation. It also involves a loan or gift of consciousness that is passed on in the context of human relationships — especially those with therapeutic or spiritual guides.

Self-awareness is also facilitated through the use of maps — maps that sum up an illuminating vision and help us to organize our observations of ourselves into an overall vision of our personality and our interpersonal relationships. In a word: "teachings."

One of these is the Psychology of Enneatypes, a body of knowledge I developed from indications in the oral tradition of the Asian Christian school that first became known in the West through Gurdjieff and later through Ichazo, and which today promises to be as useful for educators as it has been for psychotherapists over the last several decades.

It is part of wisdom, of course, that we apply the knowledge we gradually acquire regarding our life and relationships (particularly regarding our difficulties) in order to guide our steps and kindle our motivation to take corrective action. However, people's ability to learn from life is often very limited. And in order to learn *how* to learn, nothing could be better than the stimulating context of an experiential curriculum that embraces both the emotional and the instinctive dimensions of the psyche. Ideally, this would also be supported by some body-therapy, and illuminated by relevant information concerning the process of healing and transformation, along with its goals and its obstacles. There is a very close relationship between the affective and the instinctive; however much they belong to different spheres, their mutual relationship could be compared to that of the mother and the nursing infant. Indeed, how can people who have recovered a healthy love themselves not be interested in the happiness of their Inner Child?

MINDING THE INNER CHILD

I WOULD even say that in order for a cure of the heart to be wholly effective, it is essential that we also undertake the cure of what Freud used to refer to as "the vicissitudes of instinct." For healing the emotions is closely related to the undoing of what Wilhelm Reich called the bodily "character armor," and the well being that comes from being in harmony with one's spontaneous impulses seems to be a precondition for empathy. In referring to Reich's concept of body armor, however, I am not implying that we need to give priority to the specific method he developed; for the field of the "new somatologies" has developed richly since his time. These (commonly alluded to as "bodywork," "body psychotherapy," or "body therapies," and some of which could be described as the inner or subtle aspect of sports) provides future education with many resources, and it is not necessary to go into detail here about the variety of ancient and modern disciplines ranging from yoga and Tai Chi to Eutony, the Feldenkrais approach, and the Río Abierto School. In addition, the interest shown by many in the "inner game of tennis" and similar types of training is well known. Apart from their effectiveness in terms of competitive advantage, they also provide an inner psychophysical benefit: the development of a more functional, healthier attitude, and an enhanced body awareness that is relevant to emotional health and to the development of consciousness for its own sake, as in meditation.

Beyond skillful movement, even, is the health of the regulatory principle of action, for which the concept of instinct continues to be useful. And if the basic goal of affective education is the *development* of a person's potential to love — which is the key to good interpersonal relations — then healing our instinctual self may be said to involve a process of *liberation*.

Throughout the history of psychotherapy, these two aspects of the "healing of souls" have been intertwined: the liberation of spontaneity, and the awakening of love. They are parallel processes of optimization, operating in two different areas of our Self. The latter is maternal, and the former is instinctual, oriented according to the pleasure principle and the free, creative search for happiness.

In a world where goodness has become mainly normative, I think it useful to say that the development of love towards our fellow human beings can hardly go beyond an obligatory and intentional moral behavior based on control, if it cannot find support and be nurtured in a condition of caring for one's own Inner Child and his or her needs. Conversely, those who are able to heal the "vicissitudes" of their instinctive life (with its aggression and its frustrated and seemingly insatiable thirst for love) find not only the freedom of personal mental health but also an intimate satisfaction that spills over to others as warmth and empathy.

I would mistrust an education that only proposed cultivating facets of love such as solidarity and generosity without also minding its emancipatory task. I believe that the effective spiritual power of religions waned when Dionysus was relegated to a marginal position in the pantheon of the Olympian gods at the dawn of the patriarchal world, and I think Nietzsche was accurate in believing that only Dionysian spirituality could save the petrified Christian civilization. In this light, I see great promise today in the convergence between the yogic traditions of the East and the therapeutic culture of the West — which may be regarded as a cradle of Dionysus' rebirth in the contemporary world.

Becoming healthy, then, entails not just the awareness of emotional sickness and its catharsis or exorcism through expressive techniques, but also the recovery of the intrinsic health of what — in addition to the "Inner Child" — we may call the inner *animal*. Such recovery is also a liberation from psycho-cultural impediments, and an *unlearning*. It involves leaving behind childhood conditionings that originated in the parents' personalities — pervaded by the impingement of the patriarchal spirit — the "old man"* in the language of St. Paul, whose characteristics vary according to everyone's particular character neurosis.

And what a change for the better it would be for our future educators to understand that health, like freedom itself, is not so much something that is acquired, but something that people achieve by breaking out of the prison in which they have grown up without even knowing it — until they embark on the adventure of self-awareness and begin to see beyond its walls!

No matter whether we call it a "prison," an "illness," "neurosis," "sin," "*samsara*," or "ego," what matters is that we understand that the usual state of consciousness is a degraded or fragmented state of the psyche, and a kind of dream.

How inimical is this potentially liberating understanding from the accepted vocabulary of education! And yet without

---

* Just as St. Paul spoke of spiritual birth as an awakening of the "new man" within the "old man" or "old Adam," so we may say today that a new consciousness lies dormant in the "old consciousness" that we have developed during our upbringing and education in the patriarchal world.

any such concepts, we are condemned to "normosis."*

The "emotional plague" that Reich spoke of as something handed down through the generations is nothing other than the "original sin" that theologians of old attributed to genetic transmission, and what we can understand today as cultural contagion. Thus, although it has been a merit of our culture to understand the excesses of Puritanism and, more broadly, the sexual repression of the Judeo-Christian world, it is to be regretted that it has become either too conservative or too anachronistic to speak of "sin" or even "neurosis" (as was customary in Freud's day).

Yet it would be more than appropriate for teachers if they were to gain an experiential understanding of the universal myth of the hero who conquers the "dragon" of the lower self, so that they might draw their students' attention to the notion of a "holy war" against that inner "ogre" — which, as in the fairy tales, holds the "Princess" of our innermost soul imprisoned, or the treasure of our existence in its claws.

But better still: would it not be a wonderful option for students to be presented at every step in their school years with the opportunity of an experiential course that helped them not only to become conscious of their inner life but also at the same time to transcend those destructive emotions, which the Christian tradition calls the "cardinal sins," and which Indian spirituality calls "the *kleshas*"? Unfortunately, such a project is scarcely compatible with the taboos on psychotherapy and religion in the educational environment; and these, in turn, betray our ignorance, if not a lack of care for the young. In this

---

* A term introduced by Pierre Weil, the founder of Brasilia's Peace University, to designate a condition of sickness comparable to but less obvious than neurosis or psychosis.

matter, I think Eda LeShan was more lucid than most when she wrote in the late 1960s, in *Conspiracy Against Childhood*:

> Never before in history and nowhere else in the world has so much time, energy, attention and money been devoted to raising children as here in the U.S. Collectively as a nation, we invest billions of dollars every year in services for children. Individually as parents, we do not pay as much attention to anything as our own children's welfare.
>
> There are more child specialists — teachers, psychologists, psychiatrists, social workers, pediatricians, pediatric nurses, counselors, school principals, recreation leaders and parent educators — who devote their lives to the welfare of children than in any other country in the world. Thousands of husbands and fathers spend three hours or more of their working day traveling between home and work so they can afford suburban schools and more space for them to play, while a similar number of wives and mothers are marginalized from the adult world while they guide their children from one "important experience" to another, providing them with dance, music and art classes, Scout meetings, parties, puppet shows, taking them to museums and zoos, beaches, historic sites or picnics, swimming, sailing or tennis lessons, children's theater or the latest Walt Disney film. Our children have more toys, musical instruments, cars, boats, clothes, cassette recorders, radios, record players, records, books, bicycles, skis, surfboards, sleds, slides, TVs, typewriters, sewing machines, chemistry labs and games than children have ever had anywhere.
>
> But in spite of all this and much more, who would want to be a child today? Not me. I think it is a terrible time for childhood. And if this is so in spite of how much we focus on it, we must be doing something wrong.[7]

LeShan next informs us about the rising annual rate of child suicides, psychosomatic and psychiatric problems, behavior disorders, and learning difficulties, raises the question of how to explain the discrepancy between our good intentions and bad results, coming to the conclusion is that *our concern for children is not true attention to their reality and desires, but rather something like a seductive indulgence on the part of someone who needs to be forgiven.*

In truth, we are a pedophobic culture, and our so-called love of children masks our inability to be good parents. Our self-satisfaction in the matter is a sham that hides our limited capacity for love.

Freud thought that, with his theory of the Oedipus complex, he had discovered the universal nature of parricide in people's secret mental lives. I think the Argentinian psychoanalyst Pichon-Rivière was no less right when he postulated, some twenty or thirty years ago, that infanticide is even more alienated from consciousness but no less universal. Expressed in less implausible terms, we can say that parents harm their children much more than they suspect in their sleep-walking existences, without even knowing how they infect them with the pathology of society, despite their best intentions.

Pleasure-seeking and enjoyment are salient features of the Child aspect of our mind, conceptualized by Freud as the *id*, and transformed over the years into Eric Berne's "Child" (in the same way Berne rebaptized the *superego* as the "Critical Parent"). It is obvious that patriarchal or traditional education – with its authoritarian (and even despotic) nature – implants in us a disdain for pleasure that is perpetuated in society as a type of psychic castration.

In addition to the implicit but unequivocal criminalization of pleasure and disobedience is the neglect of children's desires, which entails a message that children are not important, and which in turn becomes internalized. This is surely a major component of our collective unhappiness, along with the whole suite of complications that derive from it. This is why educational experiments in permissiveness have been so important, such as the excellent but much-maligned Summerhill experience, and those of the Active School, in which a variety of inspirations have converged. The passage from Rebecca Wild quoted earlier illustrates the therapeutic implication of making children feel that their preferences matter; and Steven Harrison has written an eloquent book, *The Happy Child: Changing the Heart of Education*, in which he argues for the primacy of happiness. On the first page of his introduction, after asking whether the only thing education aspires to is the preparation of children for their role in society, he responds by saying:

> This is certainly a good idea for society, but in the efficiency of producing citizen workers, are we missing the deeper meaning and higher purpose of learning? Have we forgotten about the spirit of the child, the purpose of this one life, the unique and fragile expression of a passionate and integrated life?

And he announces:

> This book is about a reorientation of education, a radical and fundamental realignment of the purpose of education. Can education shift from its current model of shaping children into components of economic production, and become an active experiment in optimizing the creativity of the whole child? We have been so busy educating our children that we have missed the heart of education, the creation of a happy life. A happy life, after all, is not only what we would like for our children, but for ourselves as well.

A happy person, fulfilled in the connection to friends, family, and community and in the expression of vocation, is likely to be useful and productive in life and to help weave the collective fabric of a functional society. What else should a society need from education other than the happiness of its people? What else should we demand for our children other than their happiness?[8]

An interest in the pleasure and joy of children naturally leads to an appreciation of their playful spirit, since there is little that children like so much as playing. It is important not only to draw attention to the importance of play in children's development, but also to point out how patriarchal education systematically devalues children by characteristically subjugating them in order to make them into instruments of market forces. Placing education at the service of the will of the State is intrinsically exploitive, in the priority that schools give to passing exams and competing for grades. This puts a premium on vanity and personal advantage, strips learning of pleasure, and ravages the child's natural desire to learn.

Nowadays, bombarding children with exams — a multi-million-dollar industry — appeals to the concept of "quality" that has been borrowed from the industrial world. Aside from the matter of how questionable these exams are, given the lack of correlation between tests and later performance on the job, it would be high time for educational institutions to understand that the kind of quality that matters does not lie in passing exams, but in fulfilling far more important objectives of education — such as the development of creativity, the ability to establish satisfactory relationships with others, and happiness.

Another aspect of education that lies beyond the transmission of knowledge and the nurturing of nurturance — also within the scope of educating for the freedom of the Inner Child — is spontaneity, no less inhibited by conventional education than pleasure and playfulness. It is has been an important aspect of the therapeutic endeavor to help adults recover the spontaneity lost in childhood. For it goes without saying that it is not only control that matters in life, but also the ability to *let go* of control; which is to say, the capacity for *surrender*. But why wait for therapeutic repair, when education can *prevent* the loss of contact of children from their inner nature?

Valuing pleasure, the search for happiness, and saying yes to the playful spirit and to spontaneity and surrender are part of what we may call "the Dionysian spirit." Yet more than only pleasure, spontaneity, and surrender (through which we can become attuned to the will of life itself) are implied by the Dionysian spirit. It also involves *trust* in our own nature. And it also involves freedom — an aspiration appearing on the list of values that many educators proclaim as desirable, but that would be difficult for teachers to transmit if they have not succeeded in embodying it.

Ultimately, the Dionysian spirit also provides us with the ability to *disappear* — to plunge into the mysterious dimension of life. Those with a mystic vocation or culture would recognize such self-vanishing as the key to that "dying in God" that crowns the spiritual thirst of seekers, and which lies at the heart of Christian accomplishment; but, of course, our secular culture only values self-affirmation, just as Christian culture took the image of Dionysus as a model of its devil.

One very important thing that education not only neglects in its programs but even fails to mention as a goal (along with the capacity for *presence*, or contact with one's own ongoing experience) is something that Fritz Perls called "responsibility." His meaning (as in existentialism), has become that given to the term in Gestalt Therapy: "response-ability," or the ability to respond; and we may also understand it to mean not evading the truth of our own experience, or, in other words, recognizing oneself as the author of one's own acts and words. We may say that it is from such response-ability that the ability to *encounter* derives, in which a person is disposed to relate genuinely to another. Carl Rogers, in discussing the requirements of a good therapist, surely referred to the same thing when he (somewhat euphemistically) introduced the term "congruence," emphasizing the agreement between feelings and actions. More simply, perhaps, would be to speak of "being oneself," or *authenticity*. This is one of the ways in which the word "truth" is used — though, of course, it has more commonly come to connote an agreement between certain statements and objective facts.

Since we can no longer deny that unhappiness is an obstacle to performance in the workplace, today even businesses are interested in human relations, and loving feelings such as solidarity and fraternity are recognized as relevant to profit. But authenticity is no less important in interpersonal relationships, and I think people are unaware of this — or that, without it, there is no suitable basis for true love of one's fellow human beings. Out of my decades of involvement in the world of human relations, I have become convinced that it is fundamental to cultivate authenticity as an antidote to the generalized falsification intrinsic both to the neurotic mind and the cultural pathology that surrounds us. Without authenticity, even *extolling* values automatically stimulates the cultivation of false, compulsive values, echoing the relationships of obedient and seductive children towards unsatisfactory parents.

No matter how much our culture has traditionally praised sincerity and honesty, I think that what has contributed most to their fostering is psychotherapy, which — along with art — has planted seeds of independent thought in the world, as well as the capacity for intimacy and islands of community. But "being oneself" does not go along very well with the "neo-Bidermeier"* spirit in our day of Newspeak[†] and the politically correct.

Decades ago, Winnicott showed that, as children in the context of our early relationship with our mothers, our developmental task was to learn to "be ourselves in the company of others." But, he also noted, people rarely acquire such spontaneity in their relational lives. In view of this, when considering the education of the future, the "laboratory of human relations" that I have been proposing (one that would take into account the *observation* of interpersonal relations as well as their *optimization*) needs to be guided not only by values such as generosity and appreciation, but also by those of sincerity, freedom, and the courage to be oneself.

As I come to the end of this discussion of the neglected emancipatory aspect of education, I want to draw attention to an unfortunate vestige from childhood that is so often carried into adult life. It is quite difficult, in adult life, to rid ourselves of the education in self-rejection and lack of self-trust that we have received at home and in school. How tragically blind and ridiculous it is, therefore, to purport being interested in the self-esteem of children, while all the while we continue to disempower them and psychologically damage them through our institutional despotism. Despite the so-called democratic world, this despotism continues to deny them the freedom

---

* Bidermeier was the name given to the conventional post-Romantic culture that, in Metternich's day, followed the tempestuous period of the French Revolution and Napoleon.

[†] "Newspeak" was the term used by Orwell in his fantasy of the future, 1984, for a language in which many words (such as freedom or democracy) come to mean the opposite of what they had meant before.

of expression that the Constitution guarantees to adults, even when — in view of their need of a healthy development — it is they who need it most.

I earnestly hope, therefore, that tomorrow's educators will clearly understand that the psycho-spiritual growth so essential for the attainment of happiness entails not only self-acceptance but also *an appreciation of the goodness of nature and of what is natural.* Without such appreciation, two rapidly dwindling treasures that adorned the great civilizations before their decline — a sense of beauty and gratitude for life — become unattainable.

In his beautiful book, *The Happy Child*, Steven Harrison says:

> For those who see the child as born failed and broken, in need of repair and redirection, education will mean a revamping of the child, that is, into the child that should be. For the more sophisticated parent, the child, while not broken, needs the enlightenment of implanted values, specifically the parental values.
>
> We are all adults who "should be," and we are never enough of whatever that is. We can easily implant this essential dissatisfaction in our children and induct them into the cult of unhappiness that looks to materialism for its solace.
>
> But if we don't see children as broken at birth, then what are they if not a mystery?

I have proposed that honoring the Inner Child (whether our own or that of others) and allowing its flight is an expression of the Dionysian spirit, in the same way that giving wings to the heart is the essence of the Great Mother spirit within us; and I have shown the mutual reinforcement of these two. Yet I have gone on at greater length about the emancipatory aspect of education, because I feel that the Inner Child needs a stronger advocacy than simply compassion: after all, the cultivation of love has already been endorsed by all religious tradi-

tions. The Dionysian spirit, on the other hand, runs counter
to the patriarchal world's spirit of ascetic control. Yet this very
conflict is perpetuated by our implicitly hegemonic education.
An *integral* education, on the other hand, would promote the
kind of ecumenism that is the central theme of this book: one
in which the patristic heritage is counterbalanced by merciful
spirit (symbolized by Mary in Christian culture, but in our culture subordinated to the interests of greed), and the libertarian
Dionysian spirit, all under the aegis of the wise and peaceful
spirit of Buddhahood.

Insofar as intellectual education implies teaching, and
emotional education includes not only learning but also unlearning, an education in spontaneity involves an even greater
element of *un*learning. (This is true, in general, of the Inner
Child, whose capacity for creative improvisation involves learning to recognize one's own preferences and to express oneself.)

And here is where the emancipatory aspect of education
has its effect: if people are no longer slaves to the dead weight
of the past, their unconscious regime of inner tyranny, and
their obsolete reactions, then they may become citizens of a
truly democratic world. Perhaps nothing is more important, in
making this emancipatory education possible, than transforming the current idiotizing view of children, which the patriarchal culture instills in adults and even in teachers, into an attitude of true respect: the attitude of being open to *learn* from
them. Unfortunately, the spirit of traditional culture has been
to teach them what they supposedly need to know in order
to stop being ignorant little beasts devoid of culture. This has
perpetuated the conviction among educated people that we are
naturally imperfect, ignorant beings who therefore must acquire
something from the experts that will make us feel complete.

But I have always shared the intuition, expressed so famously by Wordsworth, that we come into this world from a paradisiacal condition;[9] and I feel that newborns already bring from their intra-uterine existence that undifferentiated, objectless consciousness that meditation pursues, while adults have lost it, and — recognizing it consciously, or unconsciously, as our fundamental condition and our true inner home — yearn for it.

Perhaps we could have learned to move among the things of this world without losing that consciousness of simply *being*, had the circumstances of our early lives not been so painful. But no matter how much we may have forgotten our original paradise, we have grown up in a world of much psychic pollution, in which even those who loved us most turned into transmitting agents of the toxic mentality of our diseased society.

I felt myself in good company when, at the age of about twenty, I read a letter by Dostoyevsky in which he expressed his conviction that children should always be told the truth. When I had a son years later, I tried to do that: and found it a difficult challenge. I was never able to give him a satisfactory explanation for those things in our lives that ultimately depended on social usages and political realities. My feeling that children should always be told the truth, I would say, has been part of a tendency to see them as more innocent than adults, and a feeling that each child born into the world is as pure as a flower that begins to open. I think it would be very good if adults could see children (even more than adults) as expressions of the Divine; and I suppose that this is what certain painters of old sought to express through the recurring theme of the Nativity. I think, for example, of Botticelli, who so powerfully evokes the greatness of the small through his contrast of a tiny image of the child Jesus and the largeness of the multitude, who — led by the emperor and the Pope — came to stand before the manger.

We have been taught to admire what is large, but not to discover the beauty of the small, or the wisdom hidden in the simple and ordinary. We have learned to listen to the voice of authority in the exaltation of sermons, in the brilliance of speeches, and in the vociferous enthusiasm of harangues. But if we want to raise beings capable of listening one day to that "small voice" through which the deity spoke to Elijah, we had better start listening to children.

I think that, in the midst of the collapse of the civilization we have known, children are being helped by the interest that many parents have developed in knowing themselves better. Yet our limited capacity for love is always militating against them as our many neurotic needs and our exaggerated trust in what purports to be "education," which includes more indoctrination than support for the development of the mind. Even so, perhaps one of the most noteworthy signs of progress in our decadent, problematic world is the consciousness of today's new children, who are so much more awakened than I remember from the time of my own childhood. It may be that children (together with the new shamans and the truly wise) constitute our most valuable collective resource. And I say this in the hope that consciously paying attention to it may make it even more real.

After addressing some of the cognitive, affective, and connotative aspects of what could be "an education for the third millennium," I now want to discuss what UNESCO may have meant with its idea of an education for *being* — and which, according to the "pyramidal model" of the mind that I have proposed, I take to be the key to a balance among our three inner selves.

THE TRANSPERSONAL AND
TRANSCENDENTAL, OR THE "DEEPER MIND"

I HAVE discussed how schooling would do well to foster the ripening of affective-relational abilities and the healing of instinctual life, while also understanding the relevance of the body as a support for development. It now remains to deal with the most delicate theme in my proposal: the spiritual. I take this to be the realm of being, beyond specific capabilities; or of consciousness itself, beyond thinking, feeling, and doing.

My use of the word "spiritual" is tentative, referring to a depth of the human mind that — according to the sapiential traditions — transcends the body and its emotions, as well as the intellectual mind, a usage congruent with that of those who refer to a sense of identity different from that of what Eastern spirituality and modern transpersonal psychology call the *ego*, or the "little I."

I might have talked about a "transpersonal level" of the mind and "transpersonal education," as some prefer, instead of resorting to the old word "spiritual," which is commonly felt to be much too discredited in the West. However, I have always avoided the expression "transpersonal." I do not care for the scientism implied in the choice, and I have a limited enthusiasm towards the U.S. group of psychologists who used the term as a name for their professional association. More often, I have spoken of an "integrative education" or an "education for being." However, rather than quibbling about the use of words — when it is evident that education needs to concern itself not only with reasoning and with self-knowledge, kindness, and freedom, but also with the kind of *virtue* that was the concern of the Greeks, the Roman moralists, and the Christians who founded the first universities in Europe — I am choosing to

give the expression "learning to be" a connotation deeper than
the behavioral or than that implied in a behavioristic interpretation of "character development."

More and more, the secular world in the modern West
favors lay education in reaction to the previous religious alternative, in view of the unpleasant aftertaste left by the apolo-
getic and propagandistic spirit of a Medieval Church, with
its hegemonic pretensions. But is it not narrow-minded to
contemplate a simple choice between lay education and traditional religious education? Cannot education address higher
consciousness without becoming entrapped in the authority
of old creeds? Cannot it find a new and creative way of addressing the need to nurture that depth of the mind on which
the meaning of life, the capacity for peace, and the subtlety of
attention depend?

Despite the automatic tendency to dogmatically equate
the term "spirit" with its specific Christian connotation, I
think that in our day of cultural synthesis it should not be difficult for educated people to agree that all religions have been
paths toward something that approximates "spiritual ripening,"
and that their founders — the great religious geniuses of history — have all been giants of the "spirit," despite their diverse
languages and ways of symbolizing.

This may be seen as valid not only in reference to the
patriarchal religions of the civilized world (which have sacralized transcendence through their intuition of a spirit beyond
the visible world), but also to tribal, matriarchal, and shamanic
religions, which sacralized nature and perceived the spiritual
as immanent in the cosmos and in human consciousness. We
could go even further, like the Sufis, who say that their activity
does not necessarily have to be recognized as "spiritual." This

clearly seems to be the case of many artists and thinkers, whose deep or elevated consciousness is expressed through their art and words, without necessarily being recognized as "spiritual" in view of the limited or conventional notions regarding spirituality in traditional religious lore.

Are there not, besides, people who — in spite of not being noted for their art or thinking — are still truly notable *for their being*? Don't we all know people who, by their virtuous absence of vanity, become somehow invisible, despite the unusual development of their minds in ways that are not simply intellectual? I am convinced that there are people whose greatness consists purely in their humanness: people who could be "masters of humanity," yet have not chosen such a role, and who — in spite of being a blessing to those near to them — are not called "spiritual."

I do not aim to philosophize about what *spirit* is, and even less do I seek to define it. I do not see it as an indispensable prerequisite for formulating an education that is oriented towards the depth of the human mind. Though it is true that pure reason considers that nothing can be undertaken without first being defined, it is also true that in the great adventure of the spirit, rigorous intellect — that is, rigid intellectualism — can be an impediment.

There is, in the Sufi lore, a story attributed to Mullah Nasruddin. Once, while working as a boatman, he was asked to take a grammarian to the opposite shore of a large river. Time and again, the scholarly passenger noted the errors in simple Nasruddin's speech, and finally asked him if he had ever studied grammar. To Nasruddin's reply that he had not, the grammarian remarked, "But then you have lost half of your life!" After rowing a bit more, Nasruddin asked his scholarly passenger if he had ever learned to swim; and when the latter informed him that he had not, he retorted: "What a pity. The boat has sprung a leak, and you are about to lose your *whole* life."

We do not need a precise definition of "spirit" to realize, for example, that spiritual education cannot continue being parochial — that is, dogmatic and provincial — at a time when, in our age of high technology, even the "great classic religions" seem somewhat provincial to us. Clearly, spiritual education should embrace a perspective on the religious legacy of the world, just as on the artistic legacy; but this knowledge should be trans-national, trans-cultural, and trans-systemic, along the lines of what has been proposed at the recent meetings of the Parliament of the World's Religions.

What should a spiritual education of the future be? Independently of what its core may be, it should comprise a presentation of the essence of the great spiritual traditions of humankind, as well as the lives and thinking of their highest representatives — not only Moses and Jesus Christ, but also Buddha, Lao Tze, Confucius, Mohammed, Padmasambhava, and the Hindu saints, from the Vedic times of Vyasa to Ramakrishna and Ramana Maharshi. And yet this would be but a preliminary instruction for an experiential spiritual education, which, in our day and age, could only be ecumenical and integrative.

Since we do not yet have such an intercultural spiritual laboratory, it will have to be created. And we can imagine that one reason why it has not been created thus far is that, although it would be easy to design an introductory course on the spiritual schools of different cultures on the basis of existing texts, a course in spirituality would need to be more than just a potpourri of spiritual exercises. Rather, it should be a well-organized mosaic of methods for consciousness development, derived from an accurate understanding of the traditions and the underlying issues of their techniques and methods.

No educator has yet proposed such an integrative, trans-cultural spiritual education, as far as I know. And this, I do not find surprising. Yet since I have been an avid seeker for much of my life, who has always put his search before his professional activities, not only do I find myself in a position to try it, but I have already done it: not for groups of schoolchildren, but for adults — seekers, psychotherapists, and teachers (as I will describe in the following chapter). I don't claim to be uniquely qualified for the task, but I can say from experience that it can be done by those with the appropriate background.

Before I close this chapter, however, I want to point out again how implementing the curricular supplements that I have just suggested — in the areas of self-knowledge, human relationships, spontaneity, and the cultivation of the mind beyond the intellect — could only be possible along with a corresponding simplification of the traditional instructional curriculum.

I trust that Edgar Morin's ideas about the priority of certain kinds of knowledge over mere information — as well as the use of audiovisual resources, and computer and communication technology — will make it possible to cut down the number of hours currently devoted to a scientific and social sciences curriculum. Only in this way could the students have sufficient time for the experiential curriculum that needs to be added as a supplement to traditional instruction. When this happens, teachers — freed of their overwhelming commitment to the role of repeaters — may at last find the time they need to engage in a truly educational function.

Naturally, transforming patriarchal education into a transpersonal and integrative education for human growth will have to wait until the relevant authorities get beyond the still-prevailing taboo against therapeutic and spiritual elements in education. And I imagine that the issue of the costs involved may delay that decision further. Furthermore, the project of changing today's education will need to undergo a stage of supplementing the training that teachers presently receive, whether through universities, schools, or continuing education programs. After all, today's teachers have neither the personal development nor the professional preparation to undertake such transformational education. And given the slowness of the usual paths of growth in both the therapeutic and spiritual spheres, it may be anticipated that this would require extraordinary expenses.

Here, again, apart from a workshop of spiritual exercises, I think my contributions to experiential psycho-spiritual work may be decisive. For by now these contributions have crystallized into a way of working with groups that has proven to be of unprecedented effectiveness in exceptionally brief periods of time. The components of this work have been integrated into compact, intensive modules that have become perfected over the past thirty years in several European and Latin American countries, where they are known as the "SAT Programs for Personal and Professional Development." I will say more about this in the next chapter.

CHAPTER 8

HEALING TEACHERS TO TRANSFORM EDUCATION

Merely to acquire information is not learning. Learning implies love of understanding and loving something for itself. Only when there is no compulsion can learning be possible, and compulsion adopts many forms. Is this not so? There is compulsion through influence, through attachment and through threats, through persuasive stimulation and subtle ways of recompense....

— J. Krishnamurti, *The Art of Living*[1]

I T IS ONE THING TO FORMULATE an educational ideal, and another to *transform* education, bringing this ideal into life.

It doesn't take much imagination to understand that simply formulating educational policies and curricular reforms would not be likely to change education. Just as life can only arise from life, awareness can only proceed from awareness.

Hence, the theme of this chapter: that *the key to a renewal of education lies in a renewal of the way in which teachers are educated (and, perhaps the bureaucrats of education as well)*.

To appreciate such a proposal, one has only to consider what has taken place over the course of the last decade in the area of "Values Education" in various South American countries, as well as Spain. Until a short time ago, these legislatures had proposed an education in which the explicit "vertical" curriculum would be interwoven with a "horizontal" curriculum contemplating values. This would have allowed teachers who were giving a biology or history class, for example, to simultaneously transmit to their pupils attitudes such as solidarity, peace, or freedom. This Values Education seemed a logical response to the progressive impoverishment of culture in terms of virtues and ideals, and I would call it a very noble proposal. For a while, many believed it to be a genuine solution to education's neglect of humanness. However, this vision may be said to have overlooked the extent to which much more is needed than offering teachers courses on so-called values education in order for values to actually be transmitted.

Can a person who is not cooperative transmit a cooperative spirit? Can a person who is not free teach freedom? "Values" such as solidarity, freedom, peace, or authenticity are facets of a mind that has matured, and not merely concepts that one has become familiar with after attending certain courses purporting to empower teachers to teach values.

For the ability to transmit values requires not so much specific skills as a transformation of personality, leading the individual from a kind of larval state (the ordinary human condition) to a state of health and plenitude. In the language of transpersonal psychology, this transformation involves a relative dis-identification from the ego, which in turn allows the release of the person's essential being.

Fortunately, what today's educators need in order to improve their ability to teach values coincides with what they need as human beings. Unfortunately, though, they seem not to know it. Even if something truly useful to their growth were offered to them (overloaded as they are, and all too familiar with courses that have contributed little or nothing to their own welfare or true development), they probably would perceive it as simply one more opportunity for job advancement.

Teachers from the majority of Western countries are depressed, and many suffer from psychosomatic illnesses; but mainly, they are unmotivated. Only by nurturing their emotional life,* I am convinced, could we help them regain their desire to help others. For this reason, the "improvement courses" they need are not those that have been included or known so far within traditional pedagogy. Rather, we find the relevant ingredients among the teachings of the wisdom traditions, as well as those relevant to the preparation of psychotherapists.

What teachers really need is a predominantly *experiential* school, which teaches them the vital and necessary work involved in overcoming destructive attitudes and thus cultivating the higher emotions and virtues: a school for self-knowledge and for the work of dis-identification from the conditioned personality. For only such a process might guide our future teachers towards the discovery of their true being, which is the *true* fountain of values and virtues.

_____

* I am sure that the discontent of educators — at times so difficult for them to explain, themselves — is the result of having to sell themselves on a task that fails to provide a true service to their pupils. We all need to feel that we are useful for something; and as much as we try to fool ourselves into succumbing to a systemic deceit, we languish when our lives objectively lack meaning.

Just as academia has been critical of spirituality, so has the educational establishment been critical of therapies. And since most people today are neither concerned with sinfulness nor open to the notion of being emotionally imbalanced or disturbed (which they arrogantly dismiss), there is little demand for a process that would guide them towards what they so much need: overcoming the "passions" or emotional obstructions, and cultivating emotional health.

Yet not only do teachers need this, but social welfare needs it, as well. And only a school for self-knowledge that teaches the work of dis-identification with the personality constructed in childhood could open up our future educators to the discovery of their true being — the very thing that they are unconsciously seeking and that their students are unconsciously missing.

Teachers, more than anyone, need an experiential complement to the present scientific, humanistic, and pedagogical curriculum; a novel curriculum that would comprise self-knowledge, interpersonal repair, and a spiritual culture based on lived experience (and thus free from dogmatism).

Assuming that those interested in finding such experiential curricula and methods will be happy to know that this is precisely what I have to offer (after four decades of continuous exploration), in the rest of this chapter I will describe the evolution of my work with groups — work that is now beginning to be applied to the training of teachers in Chile, Cataluña, Brazil, Italy, and Mexico.

An accurate explanation of my work would be incomplete without my saying something about its history. And since it would be also incomplete if I did not also mention its inner source, I will begin by saying that this flowed from a profound spiritual experience that was, for me, the culmination of a

year-long pilgrimage that divided my life into a "before" and
an "after."

In 1970, I came into contact with Oscar Ichazo, who said he
was a representative of a mysterious school to which Gurdjieff
had referred in his autobiography, and with which many disciples of Gurdjieff had yearned to come into contact. To make
a long story short, I will just say that Ichazo sent me out into
the desert near Arica, in the north of Chile, with instructions
for a forty-day-long retreat that would serve as a context for a
"transmission of consciousness." He guaranteed that in this
retreat I would not only find what I was looking for, but would
also know the answer to my doubts about following his guidance any further. What followed was a multi-faceted experience
of greater depth than I had conceived until then, despite my
familiarity with a number of the sacred texts of the world.

At the heart of the experience — beyond specifics such as
the awakening of the *kundalini* and a sort of alchemical process in the interior of my body — seemed to be an emptying
of myself through which everything else seemed to occur; a
self-emptying that was like the eye of an inner transformative
cyclone and the motor or vehicle of an inner voyage that led to
a spiritual birth: the beginning of a second life that I can call
the "path" proper, after years of seeking and preparation.

Months later, when I came to Santiago to visit my mother, she was so impressed by my transformation that she wanted
to follow in my footsteps; and this became for me the incentive
for bringing together a small group. Among its members were

earlier Gestalt trainees, friends, and friends of my mother, and we gathered together every day during a period of two months before my return to Berkeley, where I had settled years earlier. In the course of this time, I learned that I could teach in a way that integrated earlier apprenticeships with a new inspiration, and mostly I learnt to trust this inner guidance.

On returning to Berkeley, my first American group was formed. It also occurred almost spontaneously, after a visit to the psychology department of the University of California, where I had been invited to teach months earlier, and where I was scheduled to speak about Esoteric Christianity. Although I had already considered the idea of teaching, in my mind it was limited to gathering together a small group of seeker-friends. I did not imagine that very soon I would be coming into contact with a great many people previously unknown to me — many of whom had heard me at my U.C. talk, or had met me at a summer program offered at Stanford University, in response to the joint initiatives of Idries Shah's current representative (Bob Ornstein) and Esalen Institute.

The gatherings that took place for the next three years had a seminal influence in California at a time when it was still the Mecca of the New Age. Only later, however, would the name "SAT" and the official presentation of my work come — when it was suggested that, considering the large number of participants and the fees involved, it would be convenient to create an Institute. A lawyer whose house we contemplated buying spontaneously offered to take care for us of the necessary paperwork towards the establishment of a non-profit educational organization; and since a name had to be given to it, I chose "Seekers After Truth," whose initials form the word SAT. In addition to also being the Sanskrit word for "truth" and "being," the letters S-A-T seemed a good phonetic symbol of the trinitarian vision that had always inspired my work.*

In terms of content, this original SAT was an improvisation, yet an improvisation based on a structural vision. Firstly, I knew that I would want to bring together spirituality and psychotherapy. I also intended to include the body, as well as a theoretical panorama, along with meditation and work on the affective domain. In this, I was expecting from the outset to follow the basic scheme of Gurdjieff's work, which claimed to engage the physical, emotional, and mental spheres in a balanced manner, while emphasizing a "fourth factor": the mind in itself, beyond its cognitive, rational, and active aspects.

The implicit curriculum that would come to embody this integrative intent was to be different from the mosaic of practices that had comprised Ichazo's work in Arica. Broadly speaking, it integrated three streams of influence: Buddhist meditation; the rare composite of Christian esotericism that had reached me through Idries Shah and Ichazo; and psychotherapy.

---

*The intuition of the name came to my mind already formed as a logotype with the three superimposed letters. In the emblem of the three letters, I was pleased from the start to understand that — according to the Hebrew and Cabbalistic alphabet — the A, or Aleph, is the first letter and the T is the last. A and T sound like the transition from the open to the closed, since phonetically the T is a phoneme in which the air finds an obstruction. A is yang, and T is yin. And what better symbol for the reconciliatory principle than the serpentine S, winding between both, neither vowel nor completely consonant in its liquid continuity. Soon after, I was pleased to observe that the three letters also served well as an emblem of thesis, antithesis, and synthesis: the dialect that is in reality a trialect; the dialect of Hegel that Oscar Ichazo would later have to refine with his trialect. And I am also very pleased that the letters "TSA" are emblematic of the essential components of the universe: Time, Space, and Awareness, celebrated by Fritz Perls and incomparably explained by my later and actual master, Tarthang Tulku Rimpoche.

I had always felt that psychotherapy had the potential to constitute a path with a dignity comparable to that of Oriental spirituality. And since I would in time understand that psychotherapy is not a single path but a joint cultivation of self-knowledge and spontaneity — related in the Greek mysteries to the figures of Apollo and Dionysus — in retrospect I could say that SAT involved an attempt to integrate four spiritual paths: the Esoteric Christian that I had imbibed from Gurdjieff, Shah, and Ichazo; the Buddhist; the Dionysian; and the Apollonian.*

Yet later, when SAT became a formal program for the education of psychotherapists within a specific time frame, I implicitly chose to present it in professional and worldly terms, letting its esoteric origin be unspoken.

----

*Psychotherapy is Apollonian, in that it cultivates a purifying lucidity — a clarity that has a destructuring effect on our obsolete conditionings. On the other hand, therapy is also Dionysian — not only in that it is based on expression and communication, but in that it also entails an exploration of the depth of the mind through surrender. Psychotherapy, it seems to me, is an activity that encourages the facilitation of an organismic self-regulation and is a self-healing process based not only on gaining awareness, but also on daring to let go, surrendering and opening oneself up to the unknown. It is obvious, of course, that Dionysus is associated with pleasure; and from a certain point of view, we may say that psychotherapy has supported a restitution of pleasure to the life of a hyper-civilized world that (as I have been pointing out all along) has involved a turning against our instinctive nature. But I think the foremost greatness of the Dionysian archetype is that it represents not only the universal archetype of death and resurrection, but also the sacralization of madness. The most peculiar feature of Dionysus, in the history of religious thinking, is not death and resurrection (which are, after all, part of what Joseph Campbell has called the "monomyth of the Hero"), but the dissolution of ordinary consciousness through surrender to what may be described as a "healing madness" that involves the emergence of new order from chaos and openness to a learning process where wisdom is acquired through the living out of foolishness.

Soon after SAT was born, events occurred just as in the fairy-tales, when the newborn child is visited by a host of fairy godmothers. A strong influence came from Tarthang Tulku Rinpoche, whose impact on my own life has been the most significant one since then. Also considerable was the impact of the visits of the renowned Rabbi Zalman Schachter, and the classes given by Ch'u Fang Chu (disciple of the last Taoist patriarch), who taught us Tai Chi and the breathing practices of the circulation cycle of the "elixir."

I also invited Dhiravamsa, who at the time lived in London; and as a result of this visit, he later settled in California for some years before migrating to Spain. From the time of his first visit on, we were also provided with a good diet of Vipassana. Sri Harish Johari, an expert in Ayurvedic medicine and Indian Tantrism, also became part of the teaching staff of SAT during his last three years of activity in California; and the influence of Bob Hoffman, who was hardly known at that time, was also to significantly enrich our work.

The method that Hoffman had, until then, applied individually with his patients — geared to help individuals restore their loving capacity by repairing their relationships with their parents — inspired me to design a group process following a similar pattern. This process, which continues to be an essential part of our program, later inspired Hoffman's own later work with groups (presently known as the Hoffman Quadrinity Process) and has continued to evolve, like everything else in the integrative and ecumenical school that came to be known as "the SAT programs."

My original group in Berkeley, created in 1971, was followed by a parallel group in 1972, formed by relatives and friends of my earlier students, whom I had been unable to accommodate earlier, or who had not yet been interested when the first group started. And then a third group followed, and a fourth, and still others, in which I did not directly participate and in which my contributions were carried out by my students (in the context of a program enriched by the aforementioned visiting teachers). And since my work of those days was like a powerful influence that generated an intense enthusiasm, it touched many lives deeply and had a seminal, although deliberately invisible, influence in the Bay Area and even California.

However, I felt as if I were only the transmitter of an inspiration that was bound to last no longer than the charismatic phase of my life's journey; and when after about three years this inspiration weakened, I anticipated that — after having undergone the well-known expansive or "illuminative" phase of the inner journey — I would enter the desert of the "dark night of the soul." When I saw that it was actually beginning to happen, I decided to leave my groups to my students, so as to devote myself more to my own inner process and where life might take me.

Some fifteen years later, however, the cycle of inner contraction again led to another cycle of expansion, and my work was reborn in Spain. Since the stimulus now was the invitation by a group of colleagues to conduct a "training program for psychotherapists" in the form of a month-long summer course that would meet over three consecutive years, the outer form of what I did was to be very different from the Berkeley venture.

Just as my work in Berkeley (which had also lasted three years) had adopted the form of a series of weekly meetings punctuated by occasional weekends — a format compatible with the participants' ordinary lives — the new format was that of a highly concentrated month-long residential retreat in the desert of Almería. And while my activity in California had been an improvisation, this new SAT took the form of a program proper (in which I integrated some of the inspirations of the past with the work of collaborators, among whom were included some of the best European Gestalt therapists).

Part of the content of the early SAT had been what I came, in time, to call "the Psychology of the Enneatypes."[2] So correspondingly, part of what I now conducted in Spain was to be a laboratory of self-study, in light of the applications of the Personality Enneagrams to the understanding of personality; only this time, it would be done in a more elaborate way. In Berkeley, for instance, I had never included Ichazo's teaching on the instinct-related subtypes, nor the virtues that constitute the "antidotes" to the nine basic passions; nor had I included the exploration of irrational ideas and other important themes. Also, just as I had originally presented the earliest group applications of Hoffman's "Psychic Therapy" in Berkeley, I now recruited the collaboration of Suzy Stroke, who had by now become the main trainer in Brazil's Hoffman school, and had already integrated my own contributions into that process. I also invited the collaboration of a distinguished Latin American bodyworker and dancer, Graciela Figueroa, and Cheriff Chalakani, the Egyptian-Mexican co-creator of an elaborate form of re-birthing/reparenting. Also included among my staff were the two charismatic therapists who had invited me — Guillermo Borja from Mexico, and Dr. Antonio Asín from the Basque country, who had previously invited me to work with his therapeutic community on several occasions and now thought that this intensive program was precisely what his followers needed.

After several years of convening in a special retreat center built for us in the desert of Almería, the program migrated to Castilla, then to Barcelona, then to a monastery in a village that had been the birthplace of the Cid; then to a large house in the countryside to the north of Burgos; and from there to other countries, beginning with Italy and Brazil. Also, as time progressed, other ingredients were added to this curriculum. And while it might seem that the sum of them amounted to a whimsical potpourri, I can also say that I chose them in implicit reference to a "deep structure."*

I have been often asked about "the secret" of my work, since the results have been so remarkable; and I have sometimes said that this has been due, in part, to its powerful ingredients (the psychology of Enneatypes, the "work on the inner family," Gestalt therapy, etc.), and in part to the way in which these are combined into a whole. Yet in giving such an answer, I have taken only the curriculum into account, rather than the living school, staffed by persons whose lives were deeply affected by my own influence and who had been through the experiences that allowed them to let go of childhood resentment, to integrate the instinctual world into their own lives, and to generate inner peace. Furthermore, just as in chemistry a mixture is one thing and a synthesis yet another, not even a group of competent therapists and teachers would have amounted

----

* A variation of the "pyramidal model," to which I have already referred in explaining both the psyche and holistic education, and which I might call a "pyramidal model of the Ways to Self-realization," in reference to the "three loves" balanced by wisdom. I have explained this at length in my book, *The Patriarchal Ego*, scheduled to appear in print through Feltrinelli in Italy, and hopefully in English in the not-distant future.

to the living school that I had the privilege of conducting. For, thanks to a shared understanding of many things, there emerged from our joint work an ability to "dance together" that allowed program participants to perceive the parts of the program that we presented as facets of a living whole.

As our programs migrated from Spain to Italy, Brazil, Mexico, Argentina, Germany and other countries (even Australia), these have continued to be perfected so that the work has became ever more precise and efficient. This has made it possible for the process to be conducted in a shorter time, much as portable computers have grown ever more compact over time while simultaneously accomplishing more.

At times I have referred to the SAT school as "an ego-grinding device." Some have called it "a school of love"; others, a place where they became more themselves, more human, or more authentic; and for many, it has meant discovering the spiritual dimension of life. Most have left behind old ways of feeling and seeing things, and also have seen their lives take on a new direction. In sum, for the majority of the participants, this process has constituted a gateway to a process of transformation; and for those who are more committed and sincere, an important part of the Path.

At present, the "SAT program" consists of three modules of approximately ten days each, one every year. And as the years pass, I have had the satisfaction of hearing ever-more-substantial declarations regarding the results of the work, and ever-more-moving expressions of gratitude from the participants at the end of each of the courses.

Over and over again, the SAT program has attracted and served highly experienced therapists as well as teachers and beginners; and each of the courses has left us with the feeling that it was "almost like a miracle," both because what transpired was so extraordinarily meaningful and because of the enormous learning experience that took place within its limited time span. It could be regarded as a true experience of "initiation," in the sense that it brings people to an unknown dimension: it sets them forth on a path that — in spite of not being a predetermined one — is a process that becomes irresistible as the journeyers begin to comprehend its meaning.

Of course, I would say that the remarkable results reflect not only the merit of those who have worked seriously on themselves and the efforts of my collaborators, but also the intervention of other factors — from the providential and unrepeatable, to the "magic" created in each group by an authentic community and by the blessings of diverse spiritual lineages. I also consider this success to be an experimental confirmation of my guiding conviction *that in order to help others, we do not need extensive theoretical studies, but, rather, the experience of our own transformative journey, with its attendant progress in insight, benevolence, freedom, and well being, plus a relevant practical-experiential training and a clear vision of certain fundamental notions concerning the "inner journey."*

I believe it is not an exaggeration to say that the results have been unprecedented, and current evaluations, presently being conducted at the Universities of Oxford and Barcelona, support this impression.

An important aspect of the SAT program has been its psycho-social nature: the group of participants becomes a space of intimacy, in which all members may show themselves as they are, explore alternative forms of behavior, and discover that they are accepted and appreciated beyond their customary roles.

Yet in addition to being a place where people feel accepted and validated, the SAT process and the SAT culture contain a strong element of confrontation, so that I would say that it involves a good balance between support and a shared "holy war against the ego."

Some time ago, I invited a group of colleagues to share their impressions of how the "SAT experience" had influenced them. What struck me was their emphasis on how much the participants had appreciated the example of staff members, who — in spite of being respected professionals — continued to "work on themselves" rather than hiding behind a professional role.

Today, it is widely recognized that psychotherapy depends more on the patient-therapist relationship than on techniques or insight. Usually, what is stressed concerning the relationship between the patient and the therapist is the degree of mental health and benevolence of the therapist, which are regarded as the more relevant factors to the quality of such relation; for these permit the therapist to "contain" his or her patients in a way different from that in which their parents related to them in the past. In reflecting on the SAT experience, however, I would like to emphasize the therapeutic value of authenticity that is a characteristic feature of the SAT community, and one through which participants are able to help one another grow.

As I come to the end of this book, I want to reiterate my conviction that our diseased and crisis-ridden world calls for the help of individual transformation. A healthy society cannot be conceived without healthy individuals; and yet the need for self-realization can be satisfied only to a very limited extent by traditional means. For decades, I have sought to stimulate something like a democratization of psychotherapy — or, on a broader scale, an education that teaches people to work spiritually and psychologically on themselves. The SAT school may be described as a place where people not only learn to work on themselves, but also to help each other reciprocally in this process.

Particularly in our age of business and propaganda, I cannot stop imagining that my belief to the effect that my own work may constitute a master key for the transformation of education (and thus a precious resource toward the way out of our critical collective predicament) may sound like a blatant sales pitch, if not the expression of a messianic delusion. However, those who know me well are aware that I have never sold anything in my life until now. And I hope that the wider public comes to know me enough, through this book, to sense that what motivates me — aside from an interest in the common good — is rather a sense of responsibility towards my work, comparable to that of a father who cares about his children. And since year after year, hundreds of people who participate in my programs assure me that I have created something with a great life-favoring potential, even something that could change society through the education of educators, I have felt justified in sharing the good news.

As I intend to step back from the activity that I have generated — "with a foot already in the stirrup," as Cervantes wrote in the dedication of his *Persiles* — leaving the task of assisting the transformation of education to the efforts of others, I feel like the character of a fairytale who, in the back garden of his very own house, has discovered a magic plant whose nectar can be poison to the dragon that devastates the region.

While carrying out my usual work, I came to understand, after many years and in an apparently accidental way, that this activity — which initially seemed destined only for the benefit of my friends, and then of my psychotherapy students (and, indirectly, their patients) — could play a key part in the transformation of education. And since I was beginning to understand that it is on education that our collective destiny depends, I naturally felt like one who finds himself in possession of a precious public resource.

Yet this has not been enough to cause me to feel that I have already accomplished my task. For what is a seed, unless it is planted in a receptive terrain? Thus I have taken an interest in expressing my vision of the tragically wasted potential of education, and of my own contribution to the possible education of educators. As a result of my participation in private conversations and public conferences, I have been able to attract the interest of some governments,[3] institutions,[4] and many teachers in Europe and Latin America. Some of the latter have joined together in different countries, creating organizations whose intention is to promote and finance programs for the teaching staff of primary and secondary schools, as a supplement to the curricula in schools of education or in the context of continuous education.[5] More recently, a foundation bearing my name has arisen in Barcelona, thanks to the initiative of friends and believers in the idea so well expressed by H. G. Wells, which I have often paraphrased as, "Our future is a race between the transformation of education, and catastrophe."[6]

Let us all hope — and take it upon ourselves to ensure — that the transformation of education wins the race.

CHAPTER 9

EPILOGUE

W HEN GANDHI VISITED QUEEN Victoria and she asked him
what he thought of Western Civilization, his reply, I
have heard, was that "it would be a good idea." Throughout
this book, I have endeavored to say something similar: that
we have idealized our barbaric ways so convincingly that most
people think we have already achieved civilization; yet in doing
so, we have obscured the fact that what we have is a combination of life proper and a parasitic growth that nourishes itself
by devouring us. Or, put differently, what we have — just as in
individual existence — is half healthy growth and half pathological barbarism.

I have argued that, "material causes" aside, civilized life
was kindled by a great light, but that it also was born from
the great shadow cast by that light: a complication of religious
experience that involved the transformation of wisdom into
power, and the establishment of a right to power on behalf

of "the best" — which, in turn, led to the establishment of aristocracies, to plutocracy, and to the tyranny of demagogic politicians. I have also claimed that civilization, from its early beginnings, has rested on an unfair exercise of violence by some men who seized authority in the name of a faraway and masculine divinity, and that they gave this transcendent divinity priority over the divine immanence of human beings and the divinity of nature and its cosmic laws.

I have tried to convey that although we have learned to respect the established order, it is high time for us to recognize that civilization is pervaded by a persistent and arrogant exaggeration, much like the adolescent immaturity that persists in certain elderly people. As a result, our collective patriarchal banner has always been one of "me," "myself," "I want this," and mainly, "because I want, I must conquer."

Many things undoubtedly may contribute to healing our parasitic civilization: a less traumatic environment from birth onward, with less love-deprivation and more justice; an ethos of cultivation rather than exploitation; the unification of civil society; the humanization of the economy; and so on. Yet I have emphasized the potential contribution of *education* to the health of the soul and the spirit, which I feel is theme enough to justify a book.

I have written this book because, more than ever, I have felt a duty to share what I have come to understand. And I identify with the half-optimistic, half-alarmed attitude of Ernesto Sábato, who — writing in his article, "The Resistance" — says:

> There are days when I wake up with an absurd hope, moments in which I feel that the possibilities of a more human life are within our hands' reach. This is one of those days.
> And, so, I have sat myself down to write, almost groping in the late night, urgently, like someone who runs out into the

street to cry for help faced with the threat of a fire, or like a boat that, on the verge of vanishing, makes a last and fervent signal to a port it knows to be nearby yet is deafened by the noise of the city and by the quantity of neon signs that cloud its vision.[1]

When I wrote *The End of Patriarchy*, I used the metaphor of the hero who fights against a many-headed dragon to say that a *modern* Hercules — in contrast to the classic myth — could only triumph by aiming at the heart of civilization's beastliness. For I saw myself as one in combat against patriarchy, in emulation of the friend and mentor of my youth, Tótila Albert. But my friend's fight against patriarchy was rather archetypal and abstract, in that it seemed to take place in a world of ideals, while in the concrete world, he — the sweetest person I have known — never regarded himself as the enemy of anyone. Neither do I have the necessary aggression to make a good militant, much as I admire the heroic spirit of those who risk their lives in a common cause for justice. Aside from my not being aggressive enough to be a good fighter, what I have come to learn and practice in my life has been neither the art of the warrior nor the skill of the politician. My vocation, rather, has been that of finding my own self and of helping others free themselves of their emotional disorders, thus awakening to a greater consciousness. And now that I aim to bring my experience to the service of finding an answer to our shared *problematique*, it is natural that I continue to be a therapist — that is, a healer rather than a soldier.

I see a healer as one with a vocation for recognizing and understanding disease. And because I imagine that bringing about the health of our world will require the deep and widespread understanding of its pathological character, I hope that these pages may be a contribution to this illumination.

Aside from my practical and experiential contribution to the psycho-spiritual training of teachers, then, I hope that my vision of civilization as a psycho-spiritual accident — as well as my considerations about the inner (experiential) aspect of patriarchal culture at our historical moment, about the healing potential of education, and about Tótila Albert's ideal of a het-erarchic society — may contribute to the transformative insight that the world, in its manifest collective blindness, needs.

In our age, both the civil religion of the fatherlands and the traditional religions of the churches have lost authority, while supreme power seems to rest on the modern empire of the global economy. It is my fervent desire that the powerful ones of the world — instead of continuing to support a tradi-tional and patriarchal education that was forged at the onset of the Industrial Age as a means of conditioning the working class — may come to understand that it would be better to *actually* serve the common good, as they often have claimed they already do. For we are all "in the same boat" — and our salvation, together with theirs, is in their hands.

I do not believe that it is overly utopian to expect that an oppressive plutocracy may resolve to convert to the wholesome and holy service of the common good. Yet even if this were the case, I hope that it is not too utopian to want to influ-ence public opinion and governments so that education may change its course. Recent social changes bring to mind John Dewey, who already foresaw the need for this in his time when he pointed out that "if our education is to have any meaning for life, it must pass through an equally complete transforma-tion." He further envisioned that an education that gave the child the spirit of service and "the instruments of effective self-direction" would be "the deepest and best guarantee of a larger society that is worthy, lovely and harmonious."[2] Today, we may formulate with greater precision what is required; and the resources are at hand for a future curriculum that comprises knowledge not only of the outer world but also of the inner; and not only knowledge, but also the wisdom that is needed for emotional health and for overcoming the destructive emotions.

The Supreme Court of the U.S. currently contemplates "the inculcation of values" as a function of education. Yet we now know that values cannot be properly *inculcated*. At a relative level, of course both values and counter-values are transmitted when there is sufficient respect; however, the deeper values are part of waking up to one's true life and to the wisdom of self-realization.

I earnestly hope that the mysterious Fortune (which does not play dice but governs them) may favor the project of educational change that I propose, and that my arguments and influence may serve to turn it into a reality soon enough. For if H. G. Wells could say that *"history is a race between education and catastrophe,"* it should be clear by now that the kind of education we currently endorse and force on our young (under the mistaken assumption, or pretense, that we are offering them a great gift) is part of our problem and could never save us.

As I come to the end of this Epilogue, I want to re-state the idea with which I began this book — only now in the words of a scholar. Rushton Coulburn writes, in the preface to his book, *The Origin of Civilized Societies:*

> When the Western Society, which is to say, the peoples of the European cultural descent, obviously led the world, civilization seemed to be a condition or a quality in which that society excelled. But the faltering of Western leadership and especially the breakdown of the Western imperialist dispensation have thrown doubt upon the quality of Western civilization, and

brought into debate the substance and the concept of civilization itself.[3]

And later, at the end of the same book, he reflects:

> This book may end, therefore, with two questions about that
> history. Did the advent of civilized societies usher in an era in
> human fortunes which is merely transitional, an era in which
> there has been no securely established society but merely a se-
> ries of attempts to form societies? And, if so, will the attempts
> ultimately be successful or unsuccessful?[4]

While reason can only conjecture, we need to act. And to
act, we may need faith and intuition. My own intuition is that
nothing is so dangerous to us at present as the attachment to
the known. For as we probably felt at the time of our biological
birth, in order to be collectively born to our next evolutionary
stage, we need to plunge into unfamiliar waters.

Let me then end my book with a quotation from the first
literary work in history, *The Epic of Gilgamesh*, the Sumero-
Babylonian story of the Deluge that is echoed in the Book of
Genesis. According to the Babylonian version of the legend,
Enlil, the god of Wind, speaks to Utnapishtim, who alone has
an ear sufficiently open to hear him in the surrounding noise:

> "Men of Shurupak," he said, "tear down your house and build
> a ship, abandon your possessions and the works you find beau-
> tiful and crave, and save your life instead."

DEDICATION

Tótila Albert

Although it is customary to place the dedication of a book on its first page, in this case I thought it more fitting to leave it to the end. For only after having read all that I have written will my readers know what Tótila Albert thought and how much he has inspired my work.

In the logotype of the Institute I founded in California in 1971, the letters S-A-T mean not only what I have already explained thus far, but also the invisible influence of the friend whom I have called my spiritual father, for his spirit lives on in me. They are the initials of Tótila Albert Schneider in reverse order, as they would appear after being stamped by a seal.

Over the years, I have come to understand his message better and better; and in retrospect, I can see that the imprint of his influence on my work as a psycho-spiritual guide has been greater than it seemed as it was developing, since it emerged in a way that was implicit and "organic" rather than deliberate and reasoned. As I notice this, I feel happy to have served as a mediator of his influence on the ripening of many. More recently, however, when my attention has turned from healing individuals and educating therapists to transform the world, I can say that I do what he was bent on doing. And in writing this book, I have felt prompted not only by solidarity toward my fellow humans, but also by love toward my friend and mentor, whose seed I have carried over the decades since his passing away, much as he expected that I would.

There is a story — surely fictitious, but instructive — about a Chinese Emperor who asked Confucius' advice on the pacification of his kingdom. Confucius answered, so it is said, that to bring order into his kingdom, the Emperor would first need to pacify his province.

"But how am I to do that?" the Emperor inquired.

And the sage answered, "By bringing harmony into your palace."

"And how am I to do that?"

"By harmonizing your family."

"And how am I to bring harmony to my conflicted family?"

To this, the sage responded by pointing to the Emperor's heart. "First of all, you must find harmony within you."

May harmony come into the hearts of those who wield power today, so that some of our obstacles are made lighter and Tótila's dream of a triple embrace among our inner and outer Three becomes a reality before we deplete the earth of its life-sustaining abundance — and so we may become a wise, loving, and free human community!

ACKNOWLEDGMENTS

I began this book by saying that the stimulus for writing it came from my friend Juanjo Herrera de la Muela, who proposed that I revise *The End of Patriarchy*, which — written about 25 years earlier — had failed to take into account the global economy and my activism for the transformation of education.

I accepted not only his suggestion, but also his offer to visit me for a few days and help me in the process, though the writing that I produced for the intended revised edition in the end became two separate books: the present one and another — entitled *The Patriarchal Ego* (which appeared in Italy in April 2009, published by the Urra collection of Feltrinelli), with some pages by his own hand.

For the present English version of this book, which I originally wrote in Spanish, I feel deeply indebted to Susan Sylvester, who not only translated it but also insisted on offering it to me as a gift rather than accepting any payment for her many hours of hard work. Since I know how far she is from being wealthy, and also know that she is not a compulsive do-gooder but a truly altruistic person who treads the Boddhisatva path — and who, after being deeply touched by my writing, wanted others to be touched and nourished by it, too — I gratefully accepted her gift, with great appreciation.

I also want to mention the support of two friends who, through their assistance in other matters, have made it possible for me to attend to the revision of this English manuscript in person. During my recent stay in Europe, it was Chanti Parmentier who, through her availability to assist me as a secretary, made it possible for me to revise Susan Sylvester's translation. And in her case, I also want to acknowledge the fact that — unwilling to consider this as an ordinary job, but wanting instead to collaborate with the philanthropic intent of my writing and lectures — she has insisted in making it a donation of her time.

More recently, since my return to the U.S., it has been Robert Bragg, my friend and webmaster, who has helped me with my season's agenda — which has now been the production of videos documenting the music-related poetry of Tótila Albert. This, in turn, has allowed me to re-revise the publisher's edited text of this book, attending to her numerous suggestions, questions, and requests for clarification.

I also want to thank the three persons who have read and commented on my manuscript, to each of whom I owe encouragement, corrections, and suggestions: the sociologist and educator, Dr Rubén Bag, who now resides in France, with whom I shared it first and whose appreciation was a stimulus that probably contributed to my ability to write while travelling; the anthropologist Arno Vogel, who also provided me with the Introduction; and the philosopher-therapist and vipassana instructor, Dr. Mitchell Ginsberg, whose combination of good sense, appreciative attention, and erudition in many domains of knowledge are a delight to experience through conversation.

I also owe the present edition of my book — of course — to Naomi Rose, to whom I am indebted for her willingness to be its publisher. Though not initially a publisher but rather an experienced editor and a sophisticated writing coach helping people find their own depth through self-expression, I trusted that she would be the right person to revise my own revision of Susan's text. Yet since she, like Susan before her, was moved by its content and not only was grateful for the opportunity to read it but also expressed the wish that she might be of further help in its becoming known to the English-speaking public, I suggested that she might undertake its publication. And I am very glad that she has accepted in spite of not having published a book before, for I like the idea of having my book produced with maternal care and deep appreciation, and I want to celebrate her response, which was simply: "I am willing to learn along the way."

In response to Naomi's request, I will end these pages with the following quotation from Murshid Samuel L. Lewis, "Spiritual Dancing":

> When humanity, terrorized by conflict,
> Is faced with the ruin of civilization,
> When the power of wealth has dominated justice
> And the concept of fiction-money
> Is leading to utter destruction:
> When the Holy Spirit is driven ever further away
> As this path of ascension has again reached zenith,
> To the undoing of so much near and dear to us—
> Let us, in spite of what occurs before our eyes
> Invoke that same Divine Spirit through love and beauty,
> That we may restore order and balance to humanity.

ENDNOTES

FOREWORD BY JEAN HOUSTON

[1] Charlene Spretnak, *Lost Goddesses of Early Greece: A Collection of PreHellenic Myths* (Boston: Beacon Press, 1984), pp. 99–101.

CHAPTER 1

[1] Leonard Shlain, *Sex, Time, and Power: How Women's Sexuality Shaped Human Evolution* (NY: Viking Penguin, 2003), p. 359.

[2] I use the word *problematique*, a technical term introduced by the Club of Rome, for "the many-faceted world problem." (The Club of Rome is an international global think tank whose mission is to act as a global catalyst for change.)

[3] In *Encyclopedia of Human Problems and Resources* (Humanité, 2001).

[4] From Quevedo's satirical poem, *Don Dinero (Sir Money)*, which begins, "Poderoso Caballero es Don Dinero" ("A Powerful Knight is Sir Money").

[5] Much of what we know about many of the ancient peoples comes to us from Herodotus.

6 James DeMeo, *SAHARASIA: The 4000 BCE Origins of Child Abuse, Sex-Repression, Warfare and Social Violence in the Deserts of the Old World* (Ashland, OR: Natural Energy Works: 2006).

7 David W. Anthony, *The Horse, the Wheel and Language: How Bronze Age Riders from the Eurasian Steppes Shaped the Modern World* (NJ: Princeton University Press, 2007).

CHAPTER 2

1 Fritjof Capra, *The Turning Point: Science, Society and the Rising Culture* (NY: Bantam, 1984).

2 Riane Eisler, *The Chalice and the Blade: Our History, Our Future* (NY: HarperOne, 1988).

3 David Korten, *The Great Turning: From Empire to Earth Community* (San Francisco: Berrett-Koehler, 2006).

4 Johan Bachofen, *The Matriarchy: An Investigation on the Gynecocracy in the Old World According to Its Religious and Juridical Nature* (1861).

5 The League of the Iroquis (1851).

6 Having accomplished his mission in our solar system after a stay on Planet Mars — which had made him specially acquainted with the predicament of the unfortunate inhabitants of Earth (who were incapable of harmonizing their three brains) and already on his way towards the sacred center of the universe — Beelzebub responds to the question that Hussein puts forth as to what could help the pitiful Earthlings. After adopting a solemn attitude, he explains that only the awareness of death may save them: feeling (and not only knowing on an intellectual level) that not only they themselves but also all of those whom they know are bound to die.

CHAPTER 3

1 According to Idries Shah, his descendent, as told in "The Artillery," in Shah's book, *Caravan of Dreams* (London: The Octagon Press, 1988).

2 Claudio Naranjo, *Songs of Enlightenment: The Tale of the Hero in the Evolution of Western Poetry.*

3 Sir James George Frazer, *The Golden Bough* (Mineola, NY: Dover, 2002).

4 Joseph Campbell, *The Hero with a Thousand Faces* (NJ: Princeton University Press, 1972).

5 Leo Frobenius, *African Archives*.

6 Quoted by Joseph Campbell, in *The Masks of God*, Volume 1: *Primitive Mythology* (NY: Viking, 1959, p. 165).

7 Joseph Campbell, *The Masks of God*, Volume 2: *Oriental Mythology* (NY: Viking Penguin, 1962), p. 73.

8 *Ibid.*, p. 74.

9 As an allegory of the Christian path, Dante calls on the mercy of Mother Goddess, who has access to the supreme reality.

10 Anne Baring and Jules Cashford, *The Myth of the Goddess: Evolution of an Image.* (NY: Penguin Arkana, 1992), p. 155.

11 Joseph Campbell, *The Masks of God*, Volume 3: *Occidental Mythology* (NY: Viking Penguin, 1964), p. 7.

12 Baring and Cashford, *The Myth of the Goddess*, p. 157.

13 *Ibid.*

14 Campbell, commenting on the Great Reversal: "From what we know of the temper of early cultures, it is safe to assume that the myths, rites, and philosophies first associated with these symbols were rather positive than negative in their address to the pains and pleasure of existence. However, in the period of Pythagoras in Greece (c. 582-500? BC) and the Buddha in India (563-483 BC), there occurred what I have called the Great Reversal. Life became known as a fiery vortex of delusion, desire, violence, and death, a burning waste. 'All things are on fire,' taught the Buddha in his sermon at Gaya, and in Greece the Orphic saying 'Soma sema: The body as a tomb' gained currency at this time, while in both domains the doctrine of reincarnation, the binding of the soul forever to this meaningless round of pain, only added urgency to the quest for some means of release." *The Masks of God*, Volume 4: *Creative Mythology* (NY: Penguin, 1968).

15 Baring and Cashford, *The Myth of the Goddess*, pp. 172–73.

16 Discourse of a man with his Ba, Berlin Papyrus, Number 3024.

17 René Girard, *Violence and the Sacred*, translated by Patrick Gregory (Baltimore: Johns Hopkins University Press, 1977).

[18] Gil Bailie, *Violence Unveiled: Humanity at the Crossroads* (NY: The Cross-roads Publishing Co., 1999), p. 34.

[19] Leonard Shlain, *Sex, Time and Power: How Women's Sexuality Shaped Human Evolution* (NY: Penguin, 2003).

[20] Erich Fromm, "The Theory of Mother Right and Its Relevance for Social Psychology" (article, originally published 1934). In *Love, Sexualtiy, and Matriarchy: About Gender*, ed. by Rainer Funk (NY: Fromm International Publishing Corp., 1997).

CHAPTER 4

[1] Manuel Castells, *The Rise of the Network Society: The Information Age: Economy, Society, and Culture*, Volume 1, second edition (Malden, MA: Wiley-Blackwell, 2000).

[2] Eduardo Galeano, *Patas Arriba: La escuela del mundo al reves* (Spain: Editores Siglio XXI de Espana, SA, 2002).

[3] Theodor W. Adorno, Else Frenkel-Brunswik, Daniel Levinson, and Nevitt Sanford, *The Authoritarian Personality: Studies in Prejudice Series*, Volume 1 (NY: W. W. Norton & Company, 1993).

[4] Lawrence Britt, "The 14 Characteristics of Fascism," in *Free Inquiry Magazine* (Spring 2003).

[5] Gunnar Adler-Karlsson, "Guide to Capri Philosophical Park" (www.philosophicalpark.org).

[6] Michael Ventura, feature writer and film critic (www.michaelventura.org).

[7] Robert N. Bellah, Richard Madsen, William M. Sullivan, Ann Swidler, and Steven M. Tipton, *The Good Society* (NY: Random House, 1991).

[8] Noam Chomsky, *Failed States: The Abuse of Power and the Assault on Democracy* (NY: Henry Holt, 2006).

CHAPTER 5

[1] Genesis 3:15.

[2] "A Tri-partite Model of Masculine Hegemony (TMMH)." Discussed in Simon Baron-Cohen, *Mindblindness* (Cambridge, MA: MIT Press, 1995).

CHAPTER 6

[1] Walter Lippman, "On Designing a New Society," in *The Good Society* (with Gary Dean Best) (Edison, NJ: Transaction Publishers, 2004).

[2] Identified today as the *Chalcolithic*.

[3] Isaiah Berlin, "The Birth of Greek Individualism," in *Liberty: Incorporating Four Essays on Liberty* (NY: Oxford University Press, 1969).

[4] Based on Ralph Waldo Emerson's essay, "Self-Reliance."

[5] I am indebted to Heinz von Foerster for this concept.

[6] Cristovam Buarque, *Educacionismo, educacionista* (Brasilia, Brazil: November 2008).

[7] Amartya Sen and Bernardo Kliksberg, *Primero las Gente [First People]* (Spain: Ediciones Deusto, Planeta, 2008).

CHAPTER 7

[1] Blaise Pascal, *Pensees* (1670).

[2] Originally included in my earlier book, *The End of Patriarchy*, and more recently in *Changing Education to Change the World*.

[3] Edgar Morin, *Seven Complex Lessons in Education for the Future [Les sept saviors necessaires à l'éducation du future]* (Paris: UNESCO Publishing, 1999).

[4] Claudio Naranjo, "Cambiar la educación para cambiar el mundo," in *La Llave*; and *The End of Patriarchy* (Oakland: Amber Lotus, 1994).

[5] Claudio Naranjo, *The End of Patriarchy* and *Changing Education to Change the World*.

[6] Rebecca Wild, *Raising Curious, Creative, Confident Kids: The Pestalozzi Experiment in Child-Based Education* (Boston: Shambhala, 2000), pp. 17–18.

[7] Eda LeShan, *Conspiracy Against Childhood* (NY: Macmillan, 1971).

[8] Steven Harrison, *The Happy Child: Changing the Heart of Education* (Boulder: Sentient Publications, 2002).

[9] William Wordsworth, "Ode: Intimations of Immortality":

> Our birth is but a sleep and a forgetting:
> The Soul that rises with us, our life's Star,
> Hath had elsewhere its setting,

And cometh from afar:
Not in entire forgetfulness,
And not in utter nakedness,
But trailing clouds of glory do we come
From God, who is our home:
Heaven lies about us in our infancy....

CHAPTER 8

[1] J. Krishnamurti, *The Pocket Krishnamurti* (Boston: Shambhala Pocket Classics, 2009).

[2] In 1969, Oscar Ichazo gave a series of lectures under the sponsorship of the Chilean Psychological Association, in which he presented for the first time the essentials of what he declared to be an Oriental oral tradition on the application of the Enneagram to personality, which he called "protoanalysis." In 1970 he shared this information with a group selected by myself and John Bleibtreu, in the course of a communal spiritual retreat in the Oasis of Azapa, in the vicinity of Arica, in the North of Chile. Over the following years, I developed this conception into what I called "the Psychology of Enneatypes," which included (among other things) the description of nine fundamental character types related to the nine "passions" of protoanalysis — which include the seven cardinal sins of the Christian tradition.

Heeding Ichazo's notion that this information should not become public at the time, I asked of each participant in the SAT program to sign a written agreement to this effect. Yet this commitment to reserve was violated by some, who passed on their understanding to others, who in turn offered courses and workshops on "the Enneagram." This started a popular movement and a considerable literature, which I have regarded as my "bastard children" and generally criticized for an arrogant ignorance, repetitiveness, and mediocrity.

[3] Chile, Catalunya, Brazil, Italy.

[4] San Diego University, Department of Education and Leadership; Casa de la Ciencia, Chiapas; University of Udine, Italy.

[5] In a book published in Spain — "Cambiar la educación para cambiar el mundo" (*La Llave*, 2007) — I give an account of the remarkable results of two modules of the SAT program offered to some thirty teacher

trainers convened by Mrs. Mariana Alwyn during her post as Minister of Education in Chile.

6 Originally, "Our future is a race between Education and catastrophe."

CHAPTER 9

1 Ernesto Sábato, "La Resistencia" ("The Resistance"), in *Siempre!* Volume 47, Issue 2503 (Edicional Siempre, June 6, 2001).

2 John Dewey, *The School and Society* (NY: Dover, 2001) (originally published 1900).

3 Rushton Coulborn, *The Origin of Civilized Societies* (NJ: Princeton University Press, 1959), p. 186.

4 *Ibid.*, p. vii.

REFERENCES

FOREWORD BY JEAN HOUSTON

Spretnak, Charlene. *Lost Goddesses of Early Greece: A Collection of PreHellenic Myths*. Boston: Beacon Press, 1984.

CHAPTER 1

Anthony, David W. *The Horse, the Wheel and Language: How Bronze Age Riders from the Eurasian Steppes Shaped the Modern World*. NJ: Princeton University Press, 2007.

Bachofen, Johann (1815–1887). *The Matriarchy: An Investigation on the Gynecocracy in the Old World According to Its Religious and Juridical Nature*. 1861.

Club of Rome. A not-for-profit organization representing over 30 countries in five continents, whose essential mission is "to act as a global catalyst for change through the identification and analysis of the crucial problems facing humanity and the communication of such problems to the most important public and private decision makers as well as to the general public."

DeMeo, James. *SAHARASIA: The 4000 BCE Origins of Child Abuse, Sex-Repression, Warfare and Social Violence in the Deserts of the Old World*. Ashland, OR: Natural Energy Works: 2006. www.saharasia.org.

Herodotus (485-425 BC). The first Greek historian, and the first to make investigation and inquiry the key to history. Much of what we know about many of the ancient peoples comes to us from Herodotus.

CHAPTER 2

Briffault, Robert (1876-1948). A French novelist, historian, social anthropologist, and surgeon whose book, *The Mothers*, examined the case for matriarchy on the basis of the extant ethnological information available in his day.

Capra, Fritjof. *The Turning Point: Science, Society and the Rising Culture*. NY: Bantam, 1984.

Eisler, Riane. *The Chalice and the Blade: Our History, Our Future*. NY: HarperOne, 1988.

Engels, Friedrich (1820-1895). A German social scientist and philosopher, Engels was — along with Karl Marx — a founder of communist theory: together, they wrote *The Communist Manifesto*. Engels also edited later volumes of *Das Kapital* after Marx's death, and on his own wrote *The Origin of the Family, Private Property, and the State*.

Gimbutas, Marija. A Lithuanian-American archeologist, known for her research into the Neolithic and Bronze Age cultures of "Old Europe," a term she introduced.

Gurdjieff, George Ivanovich (1866?-1949). A Greek-Armenian mystic, teacher of sacred dances, and spiritual teacher, he introduced "The Work," connoting *work on oneself* according to the Fourth Way.

Korten, David. *The Great Turning: From Empire to Earth Community*. San Francisco: Berrett-Koehler, 2006.

Maturana, Humberto. A Chilean biologist, author of *The Tree of Knowledge* and *Patriarchy and Democracy*, he launched the topic of autopoiesis (literally, self-creation: an attempt to characterize the nature of living systems).

Montagu, Ashley (1905-1999). A British-American anthropologist and humanist, he wrote *On the Natural Superiority of Women* and other books emphasizing the biological basis of love.

Morgan, Lewis Henry (1818-1881). Author, *The League of the Iroquois*, 1851. An American ethnologist, anthropologist and writer, Morgan is best known for his work on cultural evolution and Native Americans.

Ouspensky, Peter D. (1878-1947). A Russian philosopher and seeker, known for his expositions of the early work of Gurdjieff.

Wilber, Ken. An American author who writes on psychology, philosophy, mysticism, ecology, and spiritual evolution, proposing what he calls an "integral theory of consciousness." Author of *Up from Eden: A Transpersonal View of Human Evolution*. Wheaton, IL: Quest Books, 1996.

CHAPTER 3

Bailie, Gil. *Violence Unveiled: Humanity at the Crossroads.* NY: The Crossroads Publishing Co., 1999.

Barbosa, Duarte. Author, *Description of the Coasts of East Africa and Malabar in the Beginning of the Sixteenth Century.* A Portuguese writer and trader in the 15th and 16th centuries, Barbosa traveled with Ferdinand Magellan and wrote detailed accounts of foreign cultures. Quoted by Joseph Campbell, in *The Masks of God*, Volume 1: *Primitive Mythology*. NY: Viking, 1959.

Baring, Anne, and **Cashford, Jules.** *The Myth of the Goddess: Evolution of an Image.* NY: Penguin Arkana, 1992.

Campbell, Joseph. *The Hero with a Thousand Faces.* NJ: Princeton University Press, 1972.

_____. *The Masks of God*, Volume 1: *Primitive Mythology*. NY: Viking, 1959.

_____. *The Masks of God*, Volume 2: *Oriental Mythology*. NY: Viking, 1962.

_____. *The Masks of God*, Volume 3: *Occidental Mythology*. NY: Viking, 1964.

_____. *The Masks of God*, Volume 4: *Creative Mythology*. NY: Penguin, 1968.

Childe, V. Gordon. An Australian, Childe was one of the great archaeological synthesizers, attempting to place his discoveries within a theory of prehistoric development on a wider European and world scale. He is credited with coining the terms "Neolithic Revolution" and "Urban Revolution."

Eliade, Mircea (1907–1986). A professor of comparative religion, Eliade is mostly known for his books on shamanism, yoga, and the eternal return, and for his several volumes on the history of religion.

Farrell, Warren. *The Myth of Male Power*. NY: Simon & Schuster, 1993.

Frazer, Sir James George. *The Golden Bough*. Mineola, NY: Dover, 2002.

Frobenius, Leo. *African Archives*. In *Leo Frobenius on African History, Art, and Culture: An Anthology*, edited by Leopold Sedar Senghor and Eike Haberland. Princeton, NJ: Markus Wiener, 2006.

Fromm, Erich. "The Theory of Mother Right and Its Relevance for Social Psychology," in *The Crisis of Psychoanalysis*. NY: Holt, Rinehart, & Winston, 1970. In this article, Fromm studied Bachofen's theory of matriarchy, and suggested how it could be integrated into progressive thought. Fromm especially noted Bachofen's insights on how the nature of women developed, and associated nurturing character traits with the activity of mothering.

Girard, René. *Violence and the Sacred*, translated by Patrick Gregory. Baltimore: Johns Hopkins University Press, 1977.

Illich, Ivan (1926–2002). "Hospitality and Pain." Chicago, 1987. Unpublished paper.

Naranjo, Claudio. *Songs of Enlightenment: The Tale of the Hero in the Evolution of Western Poetry*.

Shah, Idries. *Caravan of Dreams*. London: The Octagon Press, 1988.

Shlain, Leonard. *Sex, Time and Power: How Women's Sexuality Shaped Human Evolution*. NY: Penguin, 2003.

CHAPTER 4

Adler-Karlsson, Gunnar. "Guide to Capri Philosophical Park." www.philosophicalpark.org.

Adorno, Theodor W. (1903–1969). This German-born member of the Frankfurt School was an international sociologist, philosopher, musicologist, and composer.

_____; Frenkel-Brunswik, Else; Levinson, Daniel; and Sanford, Nevitt. *The Authoritarian Personality: Studies in Prejudice Series*, Volume 1. NY: W. W. Norton & Company, 1993.

Britt, Lawrence. "The 14 Characteristics of Fascism," in *Free Inquiry Magazine*, Spring 2003.

Castells, Manuel. *The Rise of the Network Society: The Information Age: Economy, Society, and Culture*, Volume 1, second edition. Malden, MA: Wiley-Blackwell, 2000.

Chomsky, Noam. *Failed States: The Abuse of Power and the Assault on Democracy*. NY: Henry Holt, 2006.

Galeano, Eduardo. *Patas Arriba: La escuela del mundo al reves*. Spain: Editores Siglio XXI de Espana, SA, 2002.

Horkheimer, Max (1895–1973). This German philosopher and sociologist was a founding member of the Frankfurt School.

Ventura, Michael. This feature writer and film critic wrote a biweekly column, "Letters at 3 am," published by the *Austin Chronicle* since 1993. www.michaelventura.org.

CHAPTER 5

Baron-Cohen, Simon. Author, *Mindblindness*. Cambridge, MA: MIT Press, 1995. A professor of developmental psychopathology, he is best known for his work on autism, including his later theory that autism is an extreme form of the "male brain."

Eisler, Riane. *Sacred Pleasure: Sex, Myth, and the Politics of the Body*. San Francisco: HarperCollins, 1996.

Harmon, Willis. *Global Mind Change: The Promise of the 21st Century*. San Francisco: Berrett-Koehler, 1998.

MacLean, Paul. This American physician and neuroscientist made significant contributions in the fields of physiology, psychiatry, and brain research. His explorations have revealed the tri-partite structure of the human brain: the reptilian complex, the limbic system, and the neocortex.

Naranjo, Claudio. *Changing Education to Change the World* (in Spanish, Italian, and Portuguese versions).

_____. *The End of Patriarchy and the Dawning of a Tri-Une Society*. Oakland: Amber Lotus, 1994.

CHAPTER 6

Berlin, Isaiah. "The Birth of Greek Individualism," in *Liberty: Incorporating Four Essays on Liberty*. NY: Oxford University Press, 1969.

Buarque, Cristovam. *Educacionismo, educacionista*. Brasilia, Brazil: November 2008.

Emerson, Ralph Waldo. "Self-Reliance," in *Selected Writings*. NY: Simon & Schuster, 2009.

Kliksberg, Bernardo, and **Sen, Amartya**. *Primaro las Gente [First People]*. Spain: Ediciones Deusto, Planeta, 2008. **Bernardo Kliksberg**, an Argentinean, is one of the world's foremost experts on eradicating poverty. He has advised more than 30 countries in senior management, including several presidents and numerous public organizations and businesses. In 2005 he was awarded the Business Foundation for Sustainable Development prize. **Amartya Sen**, an Indian, is a Nobel Prize-winning economist, a trustee of Economists for Peace and Security, and a Harvard professor. He is known for his contributions to famine, human development theory, welfare economics and the foundations of poverty, gender inequality, and political liberalism. His books have been translated into more than thirty languages.

Lakoff, George. A cognitive linguist and professor of linguistics at the University of California, Berkeley, he is best known for his ideas about how metaphor influences human thinking, political behavior, and society, particularly in relation to politics.

Lippman, Walter, with Gary Dean Best. "On Designing a New Society," in *The Good Society*. Edison, NJ: Transaction Publishers, 2004.

CHAPTER 7

Berne, Eric (1910-1970). Author, *Games People Play*. An American psychiatrist who grew frustrated with the psychoanalytic approaches of his time, Berne created a new theory called Transactional Analysis, which related all interpersonal relationships to three ego-states of the individuals involved: the *Parent*, *Adult*, and *Child*.

Harrison, Steven. *The Happy Child: Changing the Heart of Education*. Boulder: Sentient Publications, 2002.

Huxley, Aldous. "The Education of an Amphibian," in *Adonis and the Alphabet: and Other Essays*. London: Chatto & Windus, 1956. The American version of this book is called *Tomorrow and Tomorrow and Tomorrow and Other Essays*. Whitefish, MT: Kessinger Publisher, 2008.

LeShan, Eda. *Conspiracy Against Childhood*. NY: Macmillan, 1971.

Morin, Edgar. Author, *Seven Complex Lessons in Education for the Future*. Paris: UNESCO Publishing, 2001. One of France's leading contemporary philosophers, Morin developed a method to reform our way of thinking. As a sociologist, his work encompasses a wide range of interests, ignoring the conventional boundaries among academic disciplines.

Parliament of the World's Religions. This organization was created to cultivate harmony among the world's religious and spiritual communities, and to foster their engagement with the world and its guiding institutions in order to achieve a just, peaceful and sustainable world. www.parliamentofreligions.org.

Pichon-Rivière, Enrique (1907–1977). An Argentinean physician, psychiatrist, and psychoanalyst whose thinking and scientific development were characterized by his efforts to redefine psychoanalysis as a social psychology.

Rogers, Carl (1902–1987). This American psychologist pioneered the person-centered approach. He was also a founder of the *humanistic* approach to psychology, and is considered one of the founding fathers of psychotherapy research.

Winnicott, D. W. (1896–1974). One of the giants of child psychiatry and analysis, Winnicott — a pediatrician and psychoanalyst — explored basic childhood relationships, especially the love bond between mother and infant, which he saw as the key to personality. His books include *Playing and Reality*, and *The Family and Individual Development*.

CHAPTER 8

Bellah, Robert N.; **Madsen, Richard**; **Sullivan, William M.**; **Swidler, Ann**; and **Tipton, Steven M.** *The Good Society*. NY: Random House, 1991.

Ichazo, Oscar. A South American student of esotericism, he founded the Arica Institute to transmit a new approach that became known for its inclusion of protoanalysis, from which Claudio Naranjo took the application of the Enneagram to the understanding of personality.

CHAPTER 9

Coulborn, Rushton. *The Origin of Civilized Societies.* NJ: Princeton University Press, 1959.

Dewey, John. *The School and Society.* NY: Dover, 2001. (Originally published in 1900.)

Sábato, Ernesto. An Argentinean novelist, journalist, and essayist concerned with philosophical and psychological issues, his political and social studies were highly influential in Argentina in the latter half of the 20th century. Author, "La Resistencia" ("The Resistance") in *Siempre!* Volume 47, Issue 2503. Published by Edicional Siempre, June 6, 2001.

TO LEARN MORE

My publisher has asked that I write an addendum to my book with information for those who may want to know more about my experiential work with groups, attend one of my events, participate in the programs that I have created, or at least see one of my videos.

Website: Perhaps all this information can be found on my website, www.claudionaranjo.net. This site lists my lecture agenda, and contains sections on "SAT" and "SAT-in Education." It also lists my publications, audio and video recordings, and other relevant materials.

Publications: As mentioned, a complete list of my other books, in English and other languages, also appears on my website. The English-language books include:
- *The End of Patriarchy*
- *The One Quest*

- *The Healing Journey*
- *The Way of Silence and the Talking Cure*
- *The Enneagram of Society*
- *Enneatypes and Psychotherapy*
- *Enneatype Structures*
- *Character and Neurosis*
- *How to Be*
- *Gestalt Therapy*
- *The Divine Child and the Hero*
- *Transformation through Insight*

Publications relevant to *Healing Civilization* (foreign-language editions):

- *Changing Education to Change the World* was written some years ago, and presently circulates in Spanish, Italian, and Portuguese. It further develops a number of themes addressed in the present book: the invisible tragedy of patriarchal education; the need for an education that is holistic and that integrates both the therapeutic and the spiritual dimensions of life; and so on.
- *The Patriarchal Mind* has appeared in Italian (under URRA — a division of Feltrinelli), and is expected to appear in Spanish within the year. I also expect it to be translated into English in the near future. This book elaborates on the psychological dimension of the same themes, particularly on the subject of the nine "social Enneatypes," or character-related social pathologies. Instead of emphasizing the specific approach to teacher education that I have developed, I undertake to present a more universal model of an "education for virtue."

Transformational education foundation in Spain: There is a *Claudio Naranjo Foundation* in Barcelona devoted to the Transformation of Education in Spain:

> *Fundación Claudio Naranjo – Por una educación integral*
> (Claudio Naranjo Foundation – for an integral education)
> Website: www.fundacionclaudionaranjo.com
> E-mail: info@fundacionclaudionaranjo.com

Internet viewing: Many video fragments have also been appearing on You Tube.

Program to take place in Europe: For an English-speaking public, I have only a seven-day program scheduled on my agenda in the English language, to take place somewhere in Europe in July 2010. If you are interested, the contact person is Dr. Katrin Reuter. Her email is: Katrin-Reuter@T-Online.de

INDEX

ABOUT THE AUTHOR

D r. Claudio Naranjo, renowned Chilean psychiatrist, writer, teacher, and internationally sought-after public speaker, is considered a pioneer for his experiential and theoretical work as an integrator of psychotherapy and the spiritual traditions. One of the earliest investigators of psychoactive plants and psychedelic therapy, and one of the three successors of Fritz Perls (founder of Gestalt Therapy) at Esalen Institute, he later

developed the Psychology of Enneatypes from Ichazo's Protoanalysis and founded the SAT (Seekers After Truth) Institute
— an integrative psycho-spiritual school. When not writing, he
travels throughout the world, dedicating his life to aiding others in their quest for transformation and seeking to influence
the public and the authorities in the idea that only a radical transformation of education could change the catastrophic
course of history.

BACKGROUND

CLAUDIO NARANJO was born on November 24, 1932, in Valpara-
iso, Chile. He grew up in a musical environment, and after an
early start at the piano he studied musical composition. Shortly
after entering medical school, however, he stopped composing,
and became more involved in philosophical interests. Important influences from this time were the Chilean visionary poet
and sculptor Tótila Albert, poet David Rosenman Taub, and
the Polish philosopher Bogumil Jasinowski.

After graduating as a Medical Doctor in 1959, he was
hired by the University of Chile Medical School to form
part of a pioneering studies center in Medical Anthropology
(CEAM) founded by Prof. Franz Hoffman. At the same time,
he served his psychiatry residency at the University Psychiatry
Clinic under the direction of Ignacio Matte-Blanco.

Involved in research on the dehumanizing effects of traditional medical education, he traveled briefly to the USA on
a mission assigned by the University of Chile to explore the
field of perceptual learning, and at that time that he became
acquainted with the work of Dr. Samuel Renshaw and with
that of Hoyt Sherman at Ohio State University.

In 1962 he was at Harvard as a Fulbright visiting scholar at the Center for Studies of Personality, and at Emerson Hall, where he was a participant in Gordon Allport's Social Psychology Seminar as well as a student of Paul Tillich. Before his return to Chile, in 1963 he became the associate of Dr. Raymond Cattell at IPAT, the Institute of Personality and Ability Testing at Champaign, Illinois, and was also invited to Berkeley, California to participate in the activities of the Center for Personality Assessment Research (IPAR). After another period at the University of Chile Medical School's Center for Studies in Medical Anthropology, Dr. Naranjo returned once again to Berkeley and to IPAR, where he continued his activities as Research Associate until 1970. It was during this time that he became an apprentice of Fritz Perls and a part of the early Gestalt Therapy community, and then began conducting workshops at Esalen Institute.

In the years that lead up to his becoming a key figure at Esalen, Dr. Naranjo also received additional training and supervision from Jim Simkin in Los Angeles, and attended sensory awareness workshops with Charlotte Selver. He became Carlos Castaneda's close friend, and became part of Leo Zeff's pioneering psychedelic therapy group (1965–66). These meetings resulted in Dr. Naranjo's contributions to the use of harmaline, MDA, ibogaine, and other phenyl-isopropyl-amines in psychotherapy — partially described in his book, *The Healing Journey*.

In 1969, he was sought out as a consultant for the Education Policy Research Center, created by Willis Harman at SRI. His report as to what was applicable to education from the domain of the psychological and spiritual techniques then in vogue was later to appear as his first book, *The One Quest*. During this same period, he co-authored a book with Dr. Robert

Ornstein on meditation (*On the Psychology of Meditation*), and also received an invitation from Dr. Ravenna Helson to examine the qualitative differences between books representative of the "Matriarchal" and "Patriarchal" orientations emerging from her factor-analytic study of fiction written for children. This led to his writing *The Divine Child and the Hero*, which was published at a much later time.

The accidental death of his only son in 1970 marked a turning-point in his life. Naranjo set off on a long pilgrimage, under the guidance of Oscar Ichazo, which included a spiritual retreat in the desert near Arica, Chile. This he considers the true beginning of his spiritual experience, contemplative life, and inner guidance.

After leaving Arica, he began teaching a group in Chile that included his mother, Gestalt trainees, and friends. This group, which began as an improvisation, shaped his activity in Berkeley in the early 1970s, which resulted in a non-profit corporation called "SAT Institute." The early SAT programs were visited by a series of guest teachers, including Zalman Schachter, Dhiravamsa, Ch'u Fang Chu, Sri Harish Johari, and Bob Hoffman.

In 1976, Dr. Naranjo was a visiting professor at the Santa Cruz Campus of the University of California for two semesters, and later, intermittently, at the California Institute of Asian Studies. Simultaneously, he also intermittently began to offer workshops in Europe. In this way he refined aspects of the mosaic of approaches in the SAT program.

In 1987, he launched a re-born "SAT Institute for personal and professional development" in Spain. Since then, the SAT program has extended with great success into Italy, Brazil, Mexico, and Argentina, and more recently into France and Germany.

Since the late 1980s, Dr. Naranjo has divided each year's agenda between his activities abroad and his writing at home in Berkeley. His many publications include the revised version of an early Gestalt therapy book, as well as three new ones. He also wrote three books on the applications of the Enneagram to personality, a new book on meditation (*The Way of Silence and the Talking Cure*), and *Songs of Enlightenment* — an interpretation of the great books of the West as expressions of "the inner journey" and variations on the "tale of the hero." And in his book *The End of Patriarchy* (the predecessor of *Healing Civilization*), he offered for the first time his interpretation of the world crisis as the expression of a psycho-cultural phenomenon intrinsic to civilization — the de-valuation of feminine nurturance and the childlike instinct on the part of our warrior culture — and offered the potential solution to this situation in the harmonious development of "three-brained" beings.

Since the late 1990s, Dr. Naranjo has attended many conferences on education, and sought to influence the transformation of the educational system in various countries. It is his conviction that "nothing is more hopeful in terms of social evolution than the collective furthering of individual wisdom, compassion, and freedom." Through his book *Changing Education to Change the World*, published in Spanish in 2004, he has sought to stimulate the efforts of teachers among SAT graduates who are beginning to be involved in a SAT-in-Education project, which offers school staff and the students in schools of education a "supplementary curriculum" of self-knowledge, relationship-repair, and spiritual culture. For such contributions, the University of Udine conferred on him an honorary Doctorate in Education in 2005.

In 2006, the Foundation Claudio Naranjo (Fundación Claudio Naranjo) was created to implement Dr. Naranjo's proposals regarding the transformation of traditional education into an education that does not neglect the human development on which he believes our social evolution depends.

Links:
    Personal website: http://www.claudionaranjo.net
    Fundación Claudio Naranjo: http://www.fundacionclaudionaranjo.com/

ABOUT ROSE PRESS

In our time of reading for information, Rose Press seeks to offer you books and other fragrant offerings that will live in your heart like an eternal time capsule, releasing their healing medicine as you need it.

"Fragrance" is not usually associated with books. Books, we tend to think, in our speeded-up age, are about ideas, entertainment, steps for helping us to be more new and improved.

And yet there have been books that are mirrors to the soul — or marvels of excavation, revealing the vast treasures hidden within. There have been books, the journey of whose reading swept readers up into their remarkable world, leaving them at the end with the passage of that journey in their bones, and the fragrance of that atmosphere still hovering invisibly near. There have been books so deeply entered into by their authors that turning the pages of these books transmitted to their readers more than a whiff of the understandings and evocations embodied in the book: they helped to form the readers' very being.

This is the vision of Rose Press books: that in taking them into yourself, you discover what is truly in you, and it opens your heart like petals opening to the light.

That said, getting to the more subtle fragrance — the distillation of more earthbound, sometimes sludgy experience — is often what book writers dream of and work in the trenches to do. Behind the most exquisite fragrance left with a reader by a book is the author's composted experience (all the years and memories and ideas and possibilities dreamed of and lived through, written and refined) that produced such perfume. So what is left on the page is the offering: the "fragrance," one might say. All the dregs have been churned up and left to sink to the bottom, leaving only the gift of the book.

This, then, is what the reader gets to experience: a hint of the churning process, but ultimately, the fragrance.

> *When 100,000 rose petals are gathered in the dark of early morning, placed into retorts filled with solvent, and heated over time until their oil rises as a liquid distillation, then you have just 1 pound of that most prized (and expensive) of aromatics, rose essence (rose absolute).*
>
> *In the same way, Rose Press books are the distillation of their authors' essence, refined over time and many revisions to bring you into contact with the gift of something fragrant and indescribably beautiful within yourself.*

Writing these books entails a journey, and reading these books is also a journey. And you, afterwards, will be the carrier of that journey in the world: burnished, more yourself than before, and smelling — even after everything — like a rose.

For other books from Rose Press, see www.rosepress.com.

QUESTIONS FOR
BOOK CLUB DISCUSSION

1. Bringing the crisis of civilization home:

The author of this book writes: "Our present crisis is nothing other than an expression of the destructive, and increasingly unsustainable, obsolescence of the imbalance that patriarchy introduced among the father, the mother and the child – in the family, in the realm of cultural values, and especially within the human mind." Discuss this in terms of your own observations, experiences, and views. How does this imbalance show up within the family? In society? Within the psyche?

2. Healing your corner of civilization:

Does Dr. Naranjo seems to agree with Freud that our civilization is built on the repression of basic human instincts? What are these instincts? What has been patriarchy's role in suppressing them? And what kinds of expression and guidance might foster their positive development?

What changes can you think of that would open our civilization to the influence of love and compassion, rather than selfishness, greed, and domination?

What recommendations of Dr. Naranjo are most relevant to you in your everyday life? Can you think of three things you could do in your present circumstances that would contribute to a more cooperative model in your own community?

3. The importance of the "Inner Family":

How might integrating the "intra-psychic family" – Father, Mother, and Child – within yourself help to heal civilization? Does it depend on the role one plays in society or is it enough to simply live an integrated life in the world as yourself? In what way(s) is the healing of civilization in your own hands, based on your reading of this book?

227

4. Working on your own "Inner Family":

How do you currently experience your "Inner Father"? Your "Inner Mother"? Your "Inner Child"?

Which aspect(s) of your Inner Family need more development and attention in order to come into balance?

How might you begin to develop this "inner person" and integrate it into a healthy Inner Family?

Aspects of the Inner Father include:
Focus... Discipline... Strength... Principles and ideals... Assertiveness... Provision... Willingness to take on challenges... Intellectual range

Aspects of the Inner Mother include:
Sympathy... Empathy... Affection... Expression of affection... Nurturing... Inwardness... Cooperation... Bonding... Attention to the needs of the immediate human environment

Aspects of the Inner Child include:
Permission to experience pleasure... Spontaneity and Play... Embodiment... Innocence and Purity... Trust... Joy

5. As a group, discuss your findings:

Are there any overlaps that emerge from one person to another? Any patterns? If so, what does this suggest about having lived in a patriarchal society, to date? What kinds of promise can be glimpsed by expanding your personal findings to a larger societal, even planetary, scale?

6. Transforming education:

What has been your experience of education, as a student? As (if applicable) an educator? Do you agree with the author that current educational institutions are designed to serve the goals of patriarchy (e.g., students' productivity, training to add to the GNP, etc.) rather than the inner being of the student? Based on your reading of this book, how might educational systems more fully value the being of children, while also preparing them to take their place in a transformed society?

TO ORDER ADDITIONAL COPIES
OF
HEALING CIVILIZATION

To Purchase

Single copies: $19.95 plus tax and shipping
Book-club and bulk orders: Special discounts available

Online

www.rosepress.com

Phone

Gateways Books and Tapes: (800) 869-0658

Special Order at local bookstores

Healing Civilization, ISBN #: 978-0-89556-163-3
Distributed by Independent Publishers Group (IPG)
(800) 888-4741